MW00659289

The Smith Wigglesworth Prophecy & the Greatest Revival of All Time

WHITAKER
HOUSE

All Scripture quotations are taken from the King James Version of the Holy Bible.

The Smith Wigglesworth Prophecy and the Greatest Revival of All Time

ISBN: 978-1-60374-554-3
eBook ISBN: 978-1-60374-676-2
Printed in the United States of America
© 2005, 2013 by Roberts Liardon

Roberts Liardon Ministries
P.O. Box 2989
Sarasota, FL 34230
E-mail: info1@robertsliardon.org
www.RobertsLiardon.com

Whitaker House
1030 Hunt Valley Circle
New Kensington, PA 15068
www.whitakerhouse.com

Library of Congress Cataloging-in-Publication Data (Pending)

No part of this book may be reproduced or transmitted in any form or by any means, electronic or mechanical—including photocopying, recording, or by any information storage and retrieval system—without permission in writing from the publisher. Please direct your inquiries to permissionseditor@whitakerhouse.com.

1 2 3 4 5 6 7 8 9 10 11 20 19 18 17 16 15 14 13

Contents

Introduction

God is not through with us yet. The Pentecostal movement that began in the Azusa Street Mission in Los Angeles in 1906 and the charismatic renewal that followed in the middle of the twentieth century are still rocking our world. The final revivals of our age will be, as all other revivals, works of the Holy Spirit. God is still working through His universal church around the world, regardless of denominational labels and personal prejudices.

The truth of the matter is, regardless of what we call ourselves as Christians, Jesus is coming back, and every day that passes brings us closer to that return. What should we be doing, and how should we be preparing, to be ready for Him?

God has never left His people without warning. While it is true that the first and best source of prophecy is God's revealed Word to us, the Bible, God has also chosen to speak to each generation of the earth through dreams and visions. This is what Peter spoke of on the day of Pentecost:

> *But this is that which was spoken by the prophet Joel; And it shall come to pass in the last days, saith God, I will pour out of my Spirit upon all flesh: and your sons and your daughters shall prophesy, and your young men shall see visions, and your old men shall dream dreams: and on my servants and on my handmaidens I will pour out in those days of my Spirit; and they shall prophesy....And it shall come to pass, that whosoever shall call on the name of the Lord shall be saved.*
>
> (Acts 2:16–18, 21)

With this in mind, and because of the great interest in the Smith Wigglesworth prophecy that was given to David du Plessis, I decided to put together this book. Why has this prophecy so caught the attention of believers worldwide? After all, this was not a prophecy given to the universal church, or even a simple body of believers, such as is recorded in the first few chapters of Revelation; it was a vision given to one minister who was then told to go and describe it to another. It was really a personal prophecy given to one man, David du Plessis. So, why all the interest?

There are a number of reasons, the foremost of which is the revival this vision foretold and its significance to the expansion of Christianity in the second half of the twentieth century. What Smith Wigglesworth saw in that vision was the charismatic renewal—a revival in the traditional denominations that had formerly rejected the Pentecostals and their "experience" to turn to and embrace that same experience, as thousands among them received the baptism of the Holy Spirit for themselves. The prophecy also spoke of the place of David du Plessis—who became known as "Mr. Pentecost"—in helping that revival to happen. In this light, it is easy to see that this prophecy is actually one of the most important events of church history in the last century, as it both foretold and catalyzed what could easily be seen as the greatest move of the Holy Spirit to date.

Echoing this is the vision given to Rev. Tommy Hicks. This vision was not to be given to only one person, as the Wigglesworth prophecy was, but it was for the body of Christ at large. It was first shared at a meeting of the Full Gospel Business Men's Fellowship, one of the prime movers of the charismatic renewal. By looking at and learning from Rev. Wigglesworth's prophecy to David du Plessis and how Rev. du Plessis walked it out, there is a good deal we can learn from looking at Rev. Hicks' vision about the end-times church and walking it out in our lifetimes.

The next great move of God does not rely on receiving new words of prophecy but taking the ones we already have and living them out. As it has often been said, whether we are the last generation on the earth or not, it is our last generation to influence our world for Jesus, and we need to be in the flow of the Holy Spirit to do so. It is not time for Him to bless our plans but for us to hook up with His plans—plans that have already been blessed from the time of creation.

As we said before, God is not through with us yet—and there is still a lot He wants us to do. Do you want to be part of that plan? Then, as you read this book, be open to what He wants to teach you, and be ready to apply these truths and live just as David du Plessis, Smith Wigglesworth, and Tommy Hicks did—"*exceeding abundantly above all that we ask or think, according to the power that worketh in us*" (Ephesians 3:20).

Smith Wigglesworth,
"The Apostle of Faith"

Part I

The Smith Wigglesworth Prophecy

1

Smith Wigglesworth and the Pentecostal Movement

When Smith Wigglesworth was born, on June 8, 1859, in the small village of Menston, Yorkshire, England, God's plans for the twentieth and twenty-first centuries were already afoot. Although the United States was on the verge of the Civil War, the Third Great Awakening was sweeping the country, renewing hunger for God and setting the stage for the Holiness Movement. At the same time in England, the changing climate of the Industrial Revolution gave way to a growing population of unemployed, homeless families. The churches of the traditional denominations chose to try to keep the destitute out of their churches, but William and Catherine Booth's Salvation Army brought revival to the streets as they preached the gospel wherever they could. In addition to this, in Wales, prayers were being raised for a new awakening of the gifts of the Holy Spirit and for God's presence to again engulf the churches. Through these movements, barriers were being removed between people hungry for God's presence in their lives, and foundations were laid for a new revelation of living by the power of God. It was time, after centuries of taking a backseat to the doctrines of men, for the Holy Spirit to fill God's people with all of His gifts in manifestation.

Smith Wigglesworth's younger years were marked by this very hunger for God, even though his parents were not yet Christians. His grandmother, however, was an old-time Wesleyan, and she always made sure, when she could, that Smith attended meetings with her.

When he was eight, he joined in with the singing at one of these meetings, and as he began, "a clear knowledge of the new birth" came to him. He realized in that moment just what the death and resurrection of Jesus meant for him, and he embraced it with his whole heart. From that day forth, he never doubted his own salvation.

Soon, he began operating as an evangelist, which would be his life's primary focus. His first convert was his own mother. When his father realized what was happening, he started taking the family to an Episcopal church. Although his father was never born again, he enjoyed the parson, who just happened to frequent the same pub as he did, and he remained a faithful churchgoer through Smith's youth.

The Wigglesworth family was poor. At the age of six, rather than starting school, Smith got a job pulling turnips in a local field. A year later, he and one of his brothers were working in a wool mill twelve hours a day. Smith's father also worked long and hard to support his wife and three sons. Because of this, Smith did not learn to read or write until much later in his life. His desire to read the Bible was so great that he finally overcame this obstacle with the guidance of his wife and the revelation of the Holy Spirit.

Smith Gets Involved with the Salvation Army

When Smith was thirteen, his family moved from Menston to Bradford, where he became deeply involved with the Wesleyan Methodist Church. Even though he couldn't read, Smith cultivated the habit of always having a copy of the New Testament with him wherever he went. Then, in 1875, when Smith was about sixteen, the Salvation Army opened a mission in Bradford, and Smith found a powerful ally in his desire to see people come to a saving knowledge of Jesus Christ. In the meetings he attended with the Salvationists, he soon learned there was great power behind prayer and fasting.

At this juncture, it is important to point out that the Salvation Army of that day was much different from the one we know today. While their work was mainly among the poor, as it is today, at that time, they saw the best thing they had to offer anyone to bring them out of poverty was Jesus Himself. Additionally, in those early years, General Booth refused to harm anyone's dignity by giving a handout, instead insisting that people either pay a small price or work for their food and lodging. The main activity of the Salvationists at that time was not opening soup kitchens and collecting clothing but holding open-air meetings, where new converts shared their testimonies and experienced believers played instruments, sang, and preached the good news of salvation. They would even form parades led by their marching bands to usher them to meeting halls.

In those early years, General Booth refused to harm anyone's dignity by giving a handout, instead insisting that people either pay a small price or work for their food and lodging.

It was not uncommon for people to come to the platform, throw themselves down on the floor, and ask God to save them, while those on stage sang praises to God. Behind all of these efforts were long hours of prayer. All-night prayer meetings were common, as was fasting. They would claim fifty or a hundred souls for the next week, and then God would bring those souls to hear the Word of God and receive salvation. Scores of people were saved through these efforts in Bradford.

At the age of seventeen, Smith met a godly man at a mill who took him in as an apprentice and taught him the plumbing trade. He also told Smith about what the Bible taught on water baptism, and soon afterwards Smith gladly obeyed and was baptized in water. During this time, he also learned more about the second coming of Christ and strongly believed that Jesus would come at the turn of the century. This made him ever more vigilant to "change the course" of everyone he met.

In 1877, at the age of nearly eighteen, Smith decided it was time to set out on his own. He went to the home of a plumber and asked for a job. When the plumber told him he had no need for any help, Smith thanked him, apologized for using his time, and turned to walk away.

Immediately, the man called him back. He said, "There is something about you that is different. I just cannot let you go."1 At that, the man hired him on the spot.

Mary Jane "Polly" Featherstone

Smith Meets Polly

Around this time, Smith also watched with great interest as a young, socially affluent woman came forward in one of the Salvation Army meetings and fell to her knees. She refused to pray with any of the workers until the speaker known as "Gypsy" Tillie Smith came and prayed with her. When they were done, the young woman jumped to her feet, threw her gloves in the air, and shouted, "Hallelujah! It is done!"

The next night, as she gave her testimony, Smith felt as if she belonged to him. As Smith later said, "It seemed as if the inspiration of God was upon her from the very first."[2] The young woman's name

1. Frodsham, *Smith Wigglesworth: Apostle of Faith*, 15.
2. Ibid., 18–19.

was Mary Jane Featherstone, but everyone called her "Polly." She eventually received a commission as an officer in the Salvation Army from General William Booth. Smith did what he could to work near her, and in the coming years, a romance bloomed between them.

By the time Smith was twenty, the man he worked for could not keep him busy anymore—he just worked too efficiently! So, Smith moved to Liverpool to find more work. There he began to minister to the children of the city. Ragged and hungry children came to the dock shed, where he preached the gospel to them and did his best to feed and clothe them from the money he made as a plumber in the area. He also visited the hospitals and ships, praying and fasting all day on Sunday, asking God for converts. As a result, he never saw fewer than fifty people saved each time he ministered. He was also frequently invited by the Salvation Army to speak at their meetings. Though he saw great results, he was never eloquent. He often broke down and cried before the people because of his burden for souls, and it was this brokenness that brought people to the altar by the hundreds.

The Smith Wigglesworth family. Front row: Ernest, Smith, Polly, and George
Back row: Alice, Seth, and Harold

As Smith and Polly grew closer, Polly eventually faced the difficult choice between continuing with the Salvation Army and pursuing her love for Smith. There were strict regulations against officers and lower ranks having romantic relationships, and even though

Smith never officially joined the Salvation Army, he was considered a private in their ranks, and Polly was an officer. So, while they would always remain true friends of the Salvationists, Polly retired from their ranks and took up mission work with the Blue Ribbon Army. Those in her Methodist Church also recognized her calling and asked her to help evangelize their churches. Hundreds were converted as a result. From the beginning, Polly had the eloquence Smith longed for but couldn't learn. Then in 1882, Smith returned to Bradford, and he and Polly wed. Polly was twenty-two years old and Smith was twenty-three.

The Bradford Street Mission Opened

Smith and Polly had a burden for a part of Bradford that had no church, so they soon opened the Bradford Street Mission and began ministering together. Polly did most of the speaking, because she was the stronger and more accomplished of the two as an orator, and Smith oversaw the needs of the rest of the work. While she preached, he was at the altar praying for more to come to Christ. Of this relationship, Smith later said, "Her work was to put down the net; mine was to land the fish. This latter is just as important as the former."[3]

In their thirty years of marriage, the Wigglesworths had five children: Alice, Seth, Harold, Ernest, and George. Before each child was born, Smith and Polly prayed over him or her, that he or she would faithfully serve God throughout life.

The winter of 1884 was very severe in Bradford, and plumbers were in high demand. As a result, a time of intense work began for Smith that would last for the next two years, and he become literally consumed by his natural occupation. His church attendance declined, and, slowly but surely, his fire for God began to

3. Frodsham, *Smith Wigglesworth: Apostle of Faith*, 22.

grow cold. In the light of Polly's increasing faithfulness, Smith's backsliding seemed all the more pronounced, to the point that her diligence began to wear on him. Then, one night, this came to a head, when she returned home from church a little later than usual. Smith confronted her, saying, "I am master of this house, and I am not going to have you coming home at so late an hour as this!" Polly quietly replied, "I know that you are my husband, but Christ is my Master."[4] At this, Smith forced her out the back door, then closed and locked it. However, in his annoyance, he had forgotten to lock the front door, so Polly simply walked around the house and came in through the main entrance, laughing. When Smith finally saw what he had done, he caught her laughter and realized how silly he had been. Together they laughed about the matter, but to Smith it was also a revelation of how cold he had grown in the things of God. Shortly afterward, he spent ten days praying and fasting in repentance, and God gloriously restored him.

The winter of 1884 was very severe in Bradford, and plumbers were in high demand. As a result, a time of intense work began for Smith that would last for the next two years, and he become literally consumed by his natural occupation.

The Ground Is Laid for the Return of Pentecost

About this same time, the National Camp Meeting Association was finding great success in the United States. American Christians were experiencing a strong knee-jerk reaction to the watering down of Scripture among academics in what was known as "higher criticism," which used human reasoning and the scientific method to throw the supernatural out of the Bible and doubted the integrity and authenticity of what was written in the Old and New testaments. The backlash came in the form of the Holiness Movement,

4. Frodsham, *Smith Wigglesworth: Apostle of Faith*, 22.

which urged Christians to accept the Word of God as it was written and cried out for a more genuine relationship and experience with God. Within its doctrines was the belief that there was more available to Christians than just salvation—believers should not only be born again but also go on to experience sanctification, a more holy and complete dedication and cleansing of one's life to live in the ways of God. Although this movement started largely among the Methodist churches, the call to holiness and sanctification soon separated traditional Methodists and other denominationalists from those seeking a deeper and fuller experience of God, and between 1893 and 1900, no fewer than twenty-three different Holiness denominations were formed. Roughly 100,000 believers left the Methodist church to join these new churches.[5] Soon the scriptural phrase "baptism with the Holy Spirit" became commonly associated with this second work of grace, called "consecration," although it was not precisely defined.

A similar renewal of the gifts of the Spirit was beginning in England. On a trip to Leeds for plumbing supplies, Smith heard of a meeting where divine healing was to be ministered. He attended and was amazed at what he witnessed. What others saw as fanaticism, Smith recognized as sincere and of God. On his return to Bradford, he would search out the sick and pay for their way to attend the Leeds healing meetings. When his wife grew ill, he told her about the meetings, somewhat afraid that she would think he had finally gone off the deep end. Instead, she agreed to go to the meetings with him. When the prayer of faith was offered for her in Leeds, she received an instant manifestation of healing. They both became passionate about the message of divine healing, and their meetings began to grow, causing them to require a larger mission space. Soon they obtained a building on Bowland Street and opened the Bowland Street Mission. Across the wall behind the pulpit, they

5. Durasoff, *Bright Wind of the Spirit: Pentecostalism Today*, 40–41.

hung a large scroll that read: "I Am the Lord That Healeth Thee."[6] Not many years after this, in the early 1900s, Smith received prayer for healing of a hemorrhoid condition he had battled since childhood. After the prayer, Smith was fully persuaded that his healing was the will of God, and he stopped taking the "salts" he had taken for the problem for many years. He soon was fully healed and never had another problem with this condition for the rest of his life.

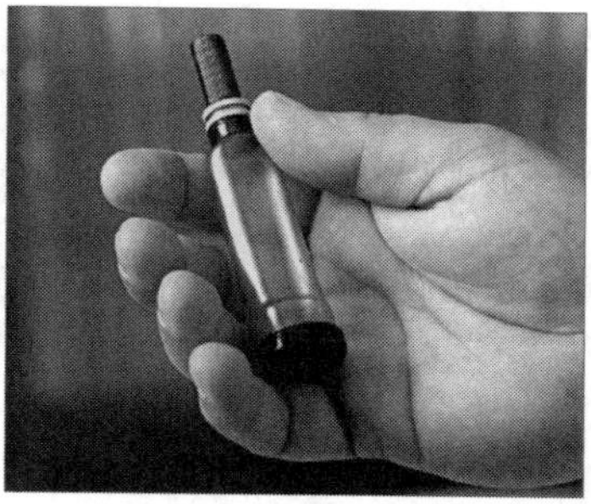

The bottle of anointing oil carried by Smith Wigglesworth

Pentecost Returns

As the twentieth century dawned, a connection of similar incidents gave way to the return of Pentecost to earth in its fullness—a movement of which Smith would eventually become somewhat of a patriarch. In December of 1900, at the close of the first term in a Bible school in Topeka, Kansas, a young preacher named Charles Parham was leading a class in studying the book of Acts. As he was about to go to Kansas City to preach, Parham asked his students to study the Bible for evidence of the baptism of the Holy Spirit and report their findings when he returned in three days. There were forty students in the class, and on the day he returned to hear their findings, he sat and quietly listened to what they had found. He was astonished at what he heard. While the accounts differed somewhat, all of the students seemed to agree that in every case, the

6. Exodus 15:26.

best and most common evidence of the baptism of the Holy Spirit was speaking in other tongues.

That evening, the group of seventy-five people was abuzz with discussion of the book of Acts as the school held its evening Watch Night Service. The meeting seemed blanketed with a spiritual freshness. Then, one of the students, a young woman named Agnes Ozman, came to Parham and asked him to lay hands on her, that she might receive the baptism of the Holy Spirit with the evidence of speaking in tongues. Parham hesitated, since he himself did not speak in tongues, but the young woman persisted. Obedient to her faith, Parham laid hands on her and prayed. As he did, Parham said, "I had scarcely repeated three dozen sentences when a glory fell on her and a halo seemed to surround her head and face, and she began speaking in the Chinese language, and was unable to speak English for three days."[7] Soon others, including Parham, received the baptism with the evidence of speaking in tongues, and the next month, he preached his first sermon on the topic so that others would know about what God was doing.

When the school building was sold unexpectedly by its owners just before the next school year, in the fall of 1901, Parham and his family moved to Kansas City. In the next few years, he would move several times. He eventually wound up in Houston, Texas, where he again ran a school in 1905. A young African-American man attended the school there, in violation of the segregation laws of Texas at the time. The young man's humility and hunger for the Word of God so moved Parham that he let the young man sit outside of the classrooms and listen to the lessons. What the young man learned of Pentecost must have had an effect, as it was he, William Seymour, who would move to Los Angeles, California, and open a mission on Azusa Street that would usher Pentecost back into the body of Christ throughout the next hundred years.

---

7. Mrs. Charles Parham, *The Life of Charles Parham*, 52–53.

The Welsh Revival

Before Azusa Street, there was one more piece God placed on the earth to prepare for the Pentecostal movement to take root. It was not enough just for men and women to again be baptized with the Holy Spirit; God also wanted to see His Spirit have free reign to minister in services as He saw fit. This began in Wales. For decades, people in Wales had been calling out for revival, and in 1904, it began. That February, a young woman named Florrie Evans stood up in a meeting and declared that she loved Jesus with all of her heart. With those words, the Holy Spirit fell on the meeting, and a fresh hunger for God spread throughout the young people in the Cardiganshire area. On September 29 of that year, Reverend Seth Joshua—who had been praying for some time that God would raise up another Elisha from an ordinary person and "mantle him with power"—led a meeting where he urged the audience to call out to God, "Bend me! Bend me!" in submission to His will. In the audience was Evan Roberts, a twenty-six-year-old hungry for God and stubborn to do nothing in ministry unless the Spirit first moved him. Evan cried this out with all of his heart, and the Holy Spirit fell on him with a deep revelation of the love of God. At least one witness said that Evan fell to the ground under this power. Evan felt impressed to return to his home in Loughor and begin a series of meetings.

In the audience was Evan Roberts, a twenty-six-year-old hungry for God and stubborn to do nothing in ministry unless the Spirit first moved him.

Those meetings began on October 31. The goal of the first meeting was to dedicate and train intercessors for the coming revival. This was successful, and soon the meetings grew to a fervor. Evan had to contact the local Bible schools to recruit more workers. The services were filled with laughing, crying, dancing, joy, and brokenness before the Lord. It was not uncommon for members of the congregation to fall to their knees in the midst of a meeting and begin praying aloud. In all things, the Holy Spirit was put first, and Evan wouldn't even rise to speak unless he felt prompted by the Spirit to do so.

In the next two years, Wales would be transformed, and more than 100,000 people would come to the Lord. Political meetings were canceled. Theatres closed for lack of attendance, as did gambling facilities and places serving alcohol. Doctrinal differences dissolved in the pursuit of God Himself, and all came together to worship and sing praises to God. Former prostitutes organized Bible studies. People began paying back long-term debts they had previously tried to ignore. Believers came from all over the world to experience what God was doing in Wales, and, as a result, the fire spread. There was no organization, set order of services, or specific location that held the revival together. Instead, it spread like wildfire based on four simple principles: 1) Confess all known sin; 2) Search out all secret and doubtful things, being sure you hold no unforgiveness in your heart; 3) Obey whatever the Holy Spirit prompts you to do; and 4) Confess the Lord Jesus openly. This hunger for God, and the presence that came with it, soon seemed to circle the globe.

The Mission at 312 Azusa Street

Hunger for God found a new home in Los Angeles when William Seymour traveled there to become an associate minister in a Nazarene Holiness church. Armed with what he had learned in Parham's school in Houston, Seymour spoke in one of his first sermons on speaking in tongues as the evidence of being baptized with the Holy Spirit. It was also his last sermon for that Nazarene congregation. He was promptly dismissed by the group as a heretic, but he found sympathetic ears elsewhere and preached in whatever home would welcome him. Black and white Americans alike gathered to hear Seymour preach, and on April 9, 1906, seven of Seymour's Baptist listeners received the Holy Spirit with the evidence of speaking in tongues. Seymour received this gift three days later, just as Parham had with his students in Kansas. In a later meeting, Jennie Moore, who later married Seymour, spoke in tongues and then walked to the piano and started playing and singing in an unknown tongue, even though she had never taken a piano lesson. Soon the numbers grew too large for any home to accommodate, and they rented a partly burned-out building in an industrial part of town. After they cleaned up the space a bit, they found that the main room—which still had sawdust on the floor from when it had been used as a stable—could hold roughly 600 people. Now they could sing and praise as loudly as they would like! The Holy Spirit fell on 312 Azusa Street like He had been unable to do in centuries, and the Pentecostal movement was born.

The Apostolic Faith Gospel Mission at 312 Azusa Street, Los Angeles, California

The Azusa Street revival would continue for the next three years in an atmosphere that must have looked much like a service in Corinth—with many of the blessings and some of the excesses that were corrected in 1 Corinthians 14—with all of the gifts of the Spirit manifesting as the Spirit willed. Conversions, baptisms, healings, and exorcisms were common. Another aspect of these meetings was that racial and denominational boundaries were ignored—all worshipped together as one in Christ. Although there were many who questioned what was happening in these services, including Parham himself, the results of these meetings were felt around the world and are still being felt today.

Smith with his daughter, Alice, who frequently traveled with him as he ministered

Smith Meets Pentecost

Meanwhile, in England, Smith's healing ministry was growing, as was his faith. Those in the Leeds Healing Home recognized Smith's faith and asked him to speak while they were away at a convention. Smith accepted only because he felt he could get someone else to do it once he was in charge of the meeting, but all others refused, insisting they felt God wanted him to speak. Smith ministered his sermon hesitantly, but, at the close of the service, fifteen people came forward for prayer, and all of them were healed! One of them had hobbled forward on crutches and began dancing around the room without them after Smith prayed for him. He had been instantly healed! No one was more surprised by the results of his prayers than Smith himself.

Another time, the wife of a devoted friend was facing death, and the doctors did not think she would make it through the night.

Smith sought ministers to come and pray for her, but he could not find anyone willing and available, so he took a friend whom he felt offered eloquent prayers, and together they went to his friend's home. However, when he asked his eloquent friend to pray, he did not pray for her healing but for the family members who would be left behind after her passing! Smith cried out for him to stop. Then he asked the husband to pray, but his prayers were no more filled with faith than the first man's. This time, Smith cried out

Smith with his daughter, Alice Salter,
at a camp meeting at Eureka Springs, Arkansas, in 1926

loudly enough to be heard in the streets: "Lord, stop him!" At that, the husband stopped, and the room fell silent. Smith then took a bottle of oil from his pocket and poured the contents over the body of the woman. At this, Smith experienced his first vision. He later described: "Suddenly the Lord Jesus appeared. I had my eyes open gazing at Him. He gave me one of those gentle smiles....I have never lost that vision, the vision of that beautiful, soft smile."[8] A few moments after the vision vanished, the woman sat up in bed, completely healed and filled with new life. She lived on to raise a number of children and even outlive her husband.

In 1907, Pentecost had reached Sunderland, and Smith heard that people there were being baptized in the Holy Spirit and speaking in other tongues. Smith felt he had to see this for himself. He

8. Frodsham, *Smith Wigglesworth: Apostle of Faith*, 35–36.

was among those who believed that sanctification and the baptism in the Holy Spirit were the same, so he felt he already had this baptism. Others warned him that the people in Sunderland were not receiving the Holy Spirit but demons instead. Other friends with whom he prayed urged him to follow his own leadings.

When Smith arrived at the meeting in Sunderland, which was being led by Vicar Alexander Boddy (who had attended some of Evan Roberts' meetings in Wales during the Welsh Revival), he was surprised at the dryness of it in contrast to the moves of the Spirit he had experienced elsewhere, especially among the Salvationists. In fact, he grew so frustrated that he interrupted the meeting, saying, "I have come from Bradford, and I want this experience of speaking in tongues like they had on the day of Pentecost. But I do not understand why our meetings seem to be on fire, but yours do not seem to be so."[9] Smith was so disruptive that they removed him from the building and disciplined him outside.

Smith opened his mouth to praise God and instantly began speaking in tongues. He knew immediately that what he had received of God now was much fuller than what he had received when praying and fasting and asking God to sanctify him.

Something about the entire issue must have stuck with him, as he went to a local Salvation Army building to pray and seek this baptism for himself. Three times while he was praying, the power of God struck him to the floor. The Salvationists there warned him against speaking in tongues, but he was determined that if it was from God, he wanted it. However, for four days he prevailed and received nothing more.

He soon decided he needed to return to Bradford, but, before doing so, he wanted to go to Vicar's home and say good-bye. There he met Mrs. Boddy and told her he was returning home without speaking in tongues.

9. Frodsham, *Smith Wigglesworth: Apostle of Faith*, 42.

She told him, "It is not tongues you need, but the baptism."[10] Smith asked her to lay hands on him before he left. She agreed, prayed a simple but powerful prayer, and then walked out of the room. It was then that the fire fell, and Smith had a vision of the empty cross with Jesus exalted at the right hand of the Father. Smith opened his mouth to praise God and instantly began speaking in tongues. He knew immediately that what he had received of God now was much fuller than what he had received when praying and fasting and asking God to sanctify him.

Instead of going home, Smith went to the church where Vicar Boddy was conducting the service and asked to speak. Vicar Boddy agreed. Smith then spoke as never before, and at the end of his "sermon," fifty people were baptized in the Holy Spirit and spoke in other tongues. Even the local paper, the *Sunderland Daily Echo*, picked up the story and headlined the meeting and what Smith had experienced. Smith telegraphed home about what had happened.

"That's Not My Smith!"

Upon arriving home in Bradford, Smith found a new challenge to what he had experienced. Polly met him at the door and firmly stated, "I want you to know that I am just as baptized in the Holy Spirit as you are, and I don't speak in tongues....Sunday, you will preach for yourself, and I will see what there is in it."[11] When Sunday came, Polly did see what there was in it, as Smith preached with a power and assurance she had never heard in him before. She squirmed in her seat, thinking, *That's not my Smith, Lord. That's not my Smith!*[12] At the end of the sermon, a worker stood and said he wanted the same experience Smith had received, and when he sat back down, he missed his chair and fell to the floor! Smith's

10. Frodsham, *Smith Wigglesworth: Apostle of Faith*, 44.
11. Ibid., 46–47.
12. Ibid.

eldest son had the same experience. In a very short while, there were eleven people on the floor, laughing in the Spirit. Then, the entire congregation was absorbed in holy laughter, as God poured even more of His Spirit out upon them. In the coming weeks, hundreds in Bradford would receive the baptism in the Holy Spirit and speak with other tongues—one of whom was Polly. The couple soon began traveling throughout the country, answering calls to speak and minister.

This experience also caused Smith to pursue God more than ever through prayer and fasting. He answered every request he could of those asking for divine healing. Sometimes he took a train to the nearest city and then borrowed a bicycle to ride another ten miles to reach the person. Soon he had no more time for his plumbing work, so he vowed before the Lord that if he were ever again in severe need, he would return to plumbing; otherwise, he would serve as a minister for the rest of his days. The Lord made sure Smith never returned to plumbing.

Polly Goes Home to Be with the Lord

Not long after this, while waiting at a train station to leave for Scotland, Smith received word that his beloved wife, Polly, had collapsed at the Bowland Street Mission from a heart attack. He rushed to her bedside, only to discover her spirit had already departed. But Smith rebuked death, and she came back. Smith had just a short time to visit with his wife, and then he was impressed that it was time for her to go home to be with her Lord and Savior, so he released her again. Polly passed away on January 1, 1913, and it was as if her dedication and spiritual power went with her husband after that and multiplied the effects of his ministry.

Immediately, Smith started to minister again throughout the country, traveling with his daughter, Alice, and her husband, James

"Jimmy" Salter. Smith continued to preach a simple gospel of "only believe." In a time when other ministers seemed frail and failing, despite the enormous revivals that had come through their ministries, Smith soon rose to prominence in Pentecostal circles because of the undeniable power in his ministry and the uncompromising stability with which he operated. It was as if Smith had no motive other than seeing Jesus glorified wherever he went, and seeing that glory kept the devil constantly on the run. He was a man moved continually by compassion from the heart of God. These convictions would never change in the next four decades, and Smith remained a growing force for God and Pentecostalism right up until his death, in 1947.

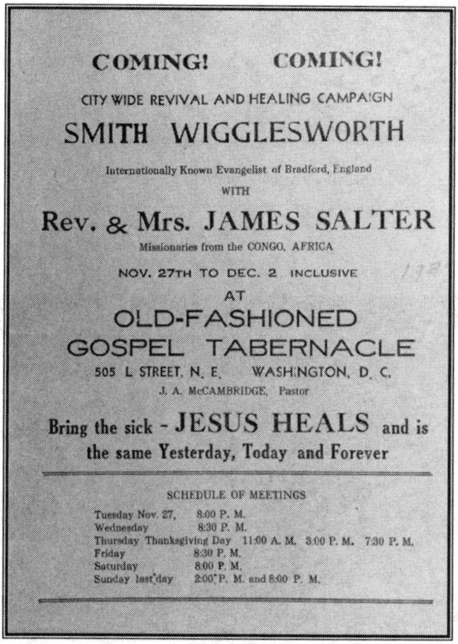

Poster announcing a revival meeting in 1934

Smith ministers the Word at Angelus Temple in Los Angeles, around 1929.

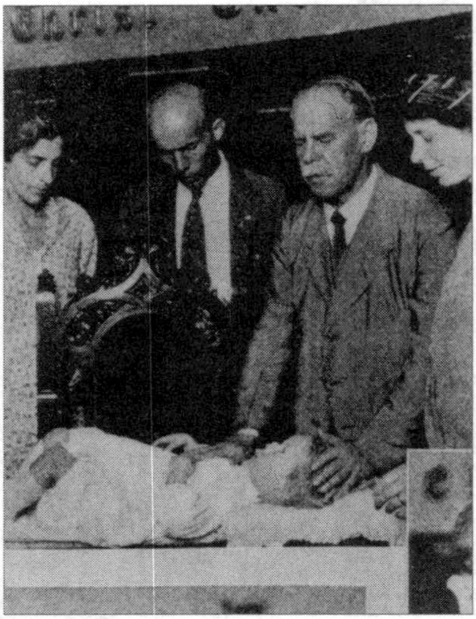

Smith laying hands on a sick child at Angelus Temple. His daughter, Alice Salter, stands to his left.

Four generations of Wigglesworths

Smith in his later years

Smith ministers in the Spirit.

Smith walking his dog on the beach in the Hove, Brighton, area of the United Kingdom in 1938

The Apostle of Faith and His Worldwide Ministry

In the months following Polly's passing, Smith's fame in England grew. In 1914, he began traveling abroad to minister. By the 1920s and 1930s, no speaker in Pentecostalism was more sought after. Although he never accepted the cloak, his acknowledgment as the "Apostle of Faith" caused the Pentecostal world to look to him as one of its greatest patriarchs, even though he had never been involved in any of the revivals that started the movement. Miracles, healings, the dead being raised, and other signs and wonders followed his ministry as he continued in the uncompromising and blunt style that no one could ever emulate. Truth be told, Smith just never seemed to feel the need to be polite when chasing out sickness, disease, and other works of the devil. His sentiment was that if the Spirit were not moving, then he would move the Spirit. This was not arrogance but confidence and faith in the work God wanted done on the earth, and this attitude always marked his ministry. Smith would simply create an atmosphere of uncompromising faith in the Word of God, and the Holy Spirit would come as if He had received a personal invitation.

Smith just never seemed to feel the need to be polite when chasing out sickness, disease, and other works of the devil. His sentiment was that if the Spirit were not moving, then he would move the Spirit.

In 1922, Smith traveled to New Zealand and Australia, among other places, and in a few short months, he saw thousands saved and several Pentecostal churches birthed in the greatest spiritual renewals either nation had ever seen. In 1936, he traveled to South Africa and delivered the famous prophecy to David du Plessis that is the subject of this book. By this time, Smith was in his seventies and was probably the best-known Pentecostal in the world. With the weight of his ministry and faithfulness behind everything he said, Smith's words of prophecy would not only change David's life but also pave the way for his work and the greatest revival the world would ever see in the charismatic renewal.

At the funeral of a fellow minister, Smith bowed his head in the midst of a conversation and went home to be with the Lord without any pain or struggle. The date was March 12, 1947, and he was eighty-seven. While Smith never formed his own denomination or wrote a book, let alone a systematic set of doctrines and theology, his simple faith still impacts believers today. Perhaps one of the greatest examples of this is the effect of a few words and his friendship in the life and ministry of David du Plessis, which we will look at in the next chapters. Yet this was not because of any special abilities that Smith had but because of his uncompromising pursuit of Jesus Christ. His relationship with God produced power that had not been seen on the earth for many centuries. For this reason, God also showed him things that others only dreamed of seeing. He never wanted to be put on a pedestal and worshipped but instead wanted to be an example of what every Christian can experience if he would "only believe."

Smith was famous for never having read anything but the Bible—primarily the New Testament—during his lifetime.

David du Plessis,
"Mr. Pentecost"

2

David du Plessis and the Charismatic Renewal

Before World War II, Pentecostalism was still regarded as a fringe movement or sect, at best—while some mainline Christian denominations ignored it, others pronounced that it was based upon false doctrine or even outright heresy. However, the movement refused to go away, and, by the latter 1940s, it began to be more widely acknowledged and tolerated. Pentecostals started to organize, looking more like mainline denominations, and they held their first World Conference in 1948. By this time, Pentecostalism was slowly passing from being considered extremism to a curiosity. Had things stayed like that, the overall body of Christ would look very different today; however, God had other plans. Events of the late 1940s and early 1950s would thrust the Pentecostal experience onto the center stage of twentieth-century Christianity for the next several decades.

One of the most noticeable of these events was the healing revival that took place in those years, involving such notable figures as A. A. Allen, William Branham, Jack Coe, Tommy Hicks, Kathryn Kuhlman, T. L. Osborn, and Oral Roberts, just to name a few. These meetings, which often took the form of large tent revivals, welcomed all attendees and created tremendous crossovers of denominational lines. Many people went away healed, but even more went away baptized in the Holy Spirit. Although the end of this healing revival was in the early 1950s, many ministries started around this time and continued strong into the 1970s and 1980s.

Para-church organizations, such as the Full Gospel Business Men's Fellowship, provided both a further stage for this spread of the Holy Spirit among denominations and financial support for ministers in this movement. From these events, the charismatic renewal began and impacted all of the old denominational churches worldwide, including the Catholic Church and many churches involved in the World Council of Churches (WCC).

Into the midst of this came a relatively unknown South African minister named David du Plessis, who not only became integral to this renewal but had been forewarned of it in a prophecy by Smith Wigglesworth in 1936. Because of David's work among the mainstream denominational churches in the 1950s, he was given the nickname "Mr. Pentecost." While others spread the baptism of the Holy Spirit, David went straight to world church leaders and explained Pentecost to them in such a way that—at least for a while—they did not try to stop the renewal. While this brought him rejection from many of the Pentecostal denominations (which we will discuss in more detail later in this chapter), it did more to throw open the floodgates of the Holy Spirit to all Christians in all denominations than the work of anyone else.

To understand the impact of his life and ministry, however, as well as the significance of Smith Wigglesworth's prophecy, it is best to go back to the beginning. David's life, upbringing, and ministry all worked together to make him the right man at the right time for the job.

David's Early Years

David Johannes du Plessis was born in a small town called Twenty-Four Rivers near Cape Town, South Africa, on February 7, 1905—just over a year before William Seymour opened the mission on Azusa Street in Los Angeles that would spark the Pentecostal revival. Like Esther of old, it seems that he was born for such a time as this.

David in his earlier years

Twenty-Four Rivers was a commune of believers that had grown out of a revival started by a Norwegian evangelist. David's father and grandfather (whose names were also David Johannes du Plessis) and their families were all members of the commune. David was the eldest of twelve children, although two of his sisters and one brother died in their youth, so he grew up as the oldest of nine brothers. His family was descended from French Huguenots—a heritage that had known persecution at the hands of the Catholic Church. The Huguenots were French Protestants who joined the Reformed Church of John Calvin in the 1500s. However, they were never accepted by the powers of France—which was strongly Catholic—and were repeatedly persecuted for their faith. The worst persecution erupted on the night of August 23, 1572, in Paris, when many of the Huguenots gathered for the wedding of Henry de Navarre, who was a Huguenot, and Marguerite de Valois, the daughter of the queen, Catherine de Medici. At the order of Catherine, French troops murdered the Huguenots wherever they were found, killing some 8,000 in what history remembers as the St. Bartholomew's Day Massacre. In the following centuries, while many of these reformers remained to stand for their faith, others fled for the hope of religious freedom in areas of the world as far-reaching as the United States and South Africa—just the type of heritage from which God would call someone to later minister to Catholics with love and forgiveness.

Ever hungry for all that God had for them, David's parents came into Pentecost in 1914 through the ministries of John G. Lake and Thomas Hezmalhalch, who had come out of the ministry of John Alexander Dowie in Zion, Illinois.[13] David's father was a simple man of self-discipline, holding as meticulously to the Scriptures and his conscience as he could. In David's autobiography, *A Man Called Mr. Pentecost,* he said that the phrase that best described his father was that of Tennyson from "The Charge of the Light Brigade"—"Theirs not to reason why, Theirs but to do and die." David Sr. held his sons to the same standards to which he held himself in everything they did. This built into David a conviction of will that would keep him humble and obedient before God for the rest of his life. David described it this way: "It instilled in me a sense of respect for my parents....If that had not been built into my character, I would not have done what the Lord commanded—and in a hurry, too. With God, a command is a command. I learned to obey immediately, exactly as I was told."[14]

One example of this conviction occurred when David was in high school. His father was a carpenter by trade, and David was helping him work on the interior of a house. David was building a door all by himself when he came across a piece of knotty wood. Rather than throwing it out, he used it with the knot against the wall so that no one could see it. As he was finishing, his father came

13. John Alexander Dowie (1847–1907) purchased 6,800 acres of farmland in Lake County, Illinois, and founded the City of Zion in 1890 as a community of faith and divine healing. For more information on the life and ministry of John Alexander Dowie, see Roberts Liardon, *God's Generals: Why They Succeeded and Why Some Failed* (Whitaker House, 1996).

14. Du Plessis, *A Man Called Mr. Pentecost*, 9.

up to inspect his work. "What happened to the piece with the knot in it?" he asked.

David responded, "I put it behind, where no one can see it."

"No one can see it?" he exploded. "The Lord can see it!" David ended up doing the entire door over again.[15]

Soon after receiving the baptism of the Holy Spirit, his father was invited to be a minister under Lake and Hezmalhalch's ministry. He applied the same rigor to living and applying the Word of God that he did to his carpentry. Soon after that, the Dutch Reformed Church told David's father and mother they had come into false teaching, and they were expelled. David saw this as one more reason the mainline denominations were not open to the truth of the gospel. Later he would describe the attitude with which he spoke against the Dutch Reformed Church as "'blind leaders of the blind.'...I thought it was my duty to 'contend for the faith.'"[16]

When Europeans were saved, noticeable change took some time to detect, yet among the Africans, changes seemed to manifest overnight.

In 1916, David's family moved to Basutoland (which was renamed Lesotho in 1966) as missionaries. The area was often called the "Switzerland of South Africa" because of the beautiful, rugged, and often snow-covered peaks. Their mission station was halfway up one of these mountains. It was here David felt he first learned about simple and sincere faith. He knew that the Africans were illiterate, yet, at the same time, much to his ten-year-old's consternation, he also realized they knew Jesus in a much more real way than he did. When Europeans were saved, noticeable change took some time to detect, yet among the Africans, changes seemed to manifest overnight. He

15. Du Plessis, *A Man Called Mr. Pentecost*, 9–10.
16. Du Plessis, *The Spirit Bade Me Go*, 11.

saw that to them, if the Bible said it one way, then that was the way it was, no questions asked. He had been getting up and praying and reading his Bible every morning for as long as he could remember, but he realized he did not know Jesus as these people did. A new cry came from his heart to know Jesus as sincerely as the Africans did.

David's Conversion and Baptism in the Holy Spirit

Later that same year, this cry of David's began to be answered. While riding from the missionary compound to the distant post office and back again on a fellow missionary's horse, David saw a thunderstorm behind him in the distance that put great fear into his heart. He decided to try to outrun the storm, but this proved futile. Soon he found himself in the midst of a downpour. Storms in Africa are often like monsoons—it doesn't just rain; water seems to fall out of the sky in solid sheets. He was about a third of the way home—an eleven-mile journey—when a lightning bolt struck the ground no more than twenty feet in front of him. Instantly, his horse stopped. Then came the deafening thunderclap. Half thrown from his horse already, he slid off the rest of the way and called out, "Jesus! Save me! Save me!"

Although no such appeal had changed him before, this call to Jesus did not go unanswered. Immediately upon his request, nothing around him had changed, but it was as if everything within had. The fear was gone, and he knew in his heart that he was saved. He looked into the sky, wondering if it would be in such clouds that Jesus would return to the earth. He wanted so strongly to meet Him face-to-face! He mounted his horse again and continued his journey. When the mail was delivered and the horse was rubbed down and dried in the barn, David returned home, where his mother asked how he had gotten through the rainstorm. His answer was simple and to the point: "Well, Jesus saved me."[17]

The following year, after the family had moved from Basutoland to Ladybrand and David's parents saw that his salvation was sincere, he was baptized in a creek by church elders. David expected that what he had read in the Bible about Jesus and also seen among the Africans in Basutoland would happen to him—that when he was immersed, he would come up out of the water speaking in tongues. He expected to be baptized both in the water and in the Spirit at the same time. Although water baptism forever changed the way he read Scripture—having been buried and raised up again in Christ, as was spoken about in Romans 6:4, he now knew that the Bible spoke directly to him as a joint-heir with Christ—he was not immediately baptized in the Spirit, as he had hoped.

A few years later, in 1918, around the age of thirteen, David decided it was time he set himself to receive the infilling of the Holy Spirit with all of his heart. While it seemed a strange request, he asked his high school principal for a day off from school so that he could spend the day in prayer. His request was granted. Because the Pentecostals were still regarded with great suspicion in the area, the only place they could rent to meet was the storehouse of a coffin maker. So, David, his father, and a half dozen others interested in helping in his quest gathered in the warehouse to fast and pray until he received this baptism. They assembled on a Thursday evening, before his day off from school, and prayed through the night, taking only a few hours for sleep. It was a creepy place in the quiet of the night, in a room with coffins stacked against the walls, but the people refused to let this deter them. They prayed all day Friday, through Friday night, and into Saturday. By this time, they were worn out, and David's nerves were fraying with frustration. At this point, a quieter youth who had gathered with them, a farm girl

17. Du Plessis, *A Man Called Mr. Pentecost*, 21–24.

about a year older than David, came and gave him a message she felt she had received from the Lord: "If you will confess the thing that is on your conscience, He will baptize you in the Holy Spirit."

Searching his conscience, David recalled a lie he had told his parents seven years prior that still troubled him. It was the first sin he had ever been aware of making. He promptly confessed this to his parents, who just as promptly forgave him. With his conscience now cleared, David returned to prayer feeling anything but worthy of being filled with God's Spirit. Yet, at this moment, he received his first vision. He saw a book, being held by two hands, whose pages were totally white and clean. Then, he heard a voice say, "There is nothing recorded against you. The blood of Jesus Christ, the Son of God, has cleansed you from all unrighteousness."[18] His heart was filled with joy at this, and he burst out in holy laughter, which soon gave way to a flow of speaking in tongues.

David eventually developed his skills and anointing as a street preacher in the weekly outdoor evangelism sponsored by his church in Ladybrand and elsewhere. In an increasingly strong and persuasive voice, he told his testimony again and again and received strong responses from all of his audiences.

David the Donkey

The last formative experience of David's youth came at a missionary conference in 1920, when he was fifteen years old. By this time, David was convinced that God was calling him into the ministry, and he asked his father if he could find an apprenticeship in one of the larger South-African cities. They decided to travel to Johannesburg, where they would first attend a missionary conference. As the conference progressed, a missionary for the northern region stood and said that he would not ask for money, because God

18. Du Plessis, *A Man Called Mr. Pentecost*, 33.

was providing all the food and other items he needed through his farming. What he did need was a donkey or two. The region where he lived was too hilly and rugged for bicycles, and horses tended to fall ill, but donkeys would be a great help in spreading the gospel in the region. After two men stood and offered him animals they could do without, David's father got to his feet, went to the front of the room, and began to speak, saying, "Well, now, it seems that we are in a very happy, giving mood. And so I would like to share with you that I also have a donkey I want to give to the Lord, but since I'm afraid he won't pull with those others, I can't send him to the missionary. But I am proud of my donkey."

David's first thought was that he didn't know of any donkey his father had. He couldn't figure out what he was talking about. He and his brothers had always wanted a donkey, but they had never owned one.

Then, his father looked back at him and said, "David, come up here." David had no idea what was going on, but he simply obeyed, as he had been taught to do. His father took him by the right ear and turned to the audience. "This is the only donkey I can give. This is my oldest son. His name is David, and he feels called to work for the Lord." He went on to explain how he and his wife had asked for a boy as their firstborn and had said they would dedicate him to the Lord. "Yes, this is the only donkey I have to give. And I'm proud to give him to Jesus."[19]

At the conclusion of the meeting, there wasn't a dry eye in the house; everyone was so moved by this act of devotion and dedication. David would later say this was the day he received his D.D. title—not his Doctorate of Divinity but "David the Donkey." It was a title he would carry with him for the rest of his life and grow to cherish, because it also symbolized his own devotion and dedication to serving the Lord.

19. Du Plessis, *A Man Called Mr. Pentecost*, 41–42.

David grew in his independence from his family (and, he suggests in his autobiography, in his stubbornness as "David the Donkey"). The only two major disagreements in his life would be between him and his father. The first came through a series of steps he took professionally. His first job in Johannesburg was as an apprentice in a print shop at the Apostolic Faith Mission (AFM) headquarters,[20] but David's aspiration went beyond the simple work as a printer toward the editorial department of the publishing shop that created and organized the text he would lay in the presses. However, the simple matter was that David did not have enough education to be an editor, which shocked him because he had always been considered a bright and capable young man. One of the brothers there approached him and suggested he get more schooling. When he went to the Lord about this, not wanting it to set back his calling to the ministry, he felt the Lord clearly tell him that though He had *called* him, He had not yet *sent* him, meaning there was still time to grow and prepare. As a result, David completed two years of basic liberal arts training at Ladybird School. It was after this that his first confrontation with his father occurred.

As a result, David completed two years of basic liberal arts training at Ladybird School. It was after this that his first confrontation with his father occurred.

David's plan was to go on and attend Grey University in Bloemfontein, but his father had seen many students lose their simple faith because of too much education, and he forbade David to go. David, however, felt that this additional schooling was essential to pave the way for his ministry, and he decided to go anyway. As a result, for a time, his father—standing firmly on 1 Timothy 3:4, which states a church leader must rule his house well—turned in his lay preacher's certificate because he could not get his eldest son to obey.

20. The AFM was the continuation of the ministry begun by John G. Lake and Tom Hezmalhalch in South Africa.

The rift was healed two years later, when David was working for the railroad in South Africa's capitol, Pretoria. Because of his position, he was able to send his father a railway ticket from Ladybrand to Johannesburg so that he could attend the AFM conference there. His father accepted. There they met privately, and when his father realized that the extra education would benefit his ministry and had not tainted his son, they again became close friends.

David's Early Years as a Minister

David had moved to Pretoria when a lack of funds prevented him from continuing school at Grey University, which he had been attending largely on student loans. When he reached his limit for borrowing on these loans, he dropped out of university and went to work for the South African Railways engineering department in order to pay them off. While there, he became a regular minister in the Upper Room, a series of rooms and a meeting hall situated above a chemist's shop just a block from the largest Dutch Reformed church in Pretoria. Since Pentecostals were still looked upon as false prophets, it was always interesting on Sundays to see the two churches emptying into the streets where the city and nation's highest officials and business leaders mingled with the poor, outrageous "apostolics."

One of the members of the congregation asked David to speak to his backslidden niece. When he met Miss Anna Cornelia Jacobs, he found out that she had had spoken a word from the Lord to one of the more distinguished women in her congregation and had been rebuked for it by the pastor. Because of this incident, she had decided not to return to church. David asked about the genuineness of her conversion, and as she told him about it, she melted and began weeping. While there had been no question about her offense, there was also no question about her love for Jesus. Before the evening was over, she was restored to the faith, and David had had a very special word from the Lord about her. The Lord simply told him, "That's your wife." Shocked, he didn't know what to make of it, but he was grateful that she was so pretty. Two days later, they went on their first date. After a courtship of eighteen months, they were married on August 13, 1927. They had seven children: Anna Cornelia[21] "Corrie" (1928–), Eunice Elizabeth (March–December 1932), David Johannes (1933–1985), Philip Richelieu (1940–), Peter Louis le Roux (1944–), Matthew Kriel (1947–), and Basel Somerset (1949–). Their marriage would last just short of sixty years.

It was his marriage that prompted David's second difference of opinion with his father, who felt that, at twenty-two, his son was too young to get married. David again stiffened and stuck to his own conviction. This time, reconciliation would not occur until David and Anna returned home with their first child. David's father melted when he met his first granddaughter. He took David aside and told him, "If you make such wise choices in everything in life as you did in the choice of a wife, you will have great success."[22] Again, their relationship was fully restored.

David and Anna's earliest years of marriage and ministry were years of learning to walk in the Spirit and to avoid temptations that could have permanently derailed their ministry.

David and Anna's earliest years of marriage and ministry were years of learning to walk in the Spirit and to avoid temptations that could have permanently derailed their ministry. In avoiding these temptations, it was a matter of choosing best over good enough. The first came on a hot summer night in Pretoria as David was preaching. He had the crowd's full

21. In an interesting side note, David's mother, wife, and first daughter all had the same name, Anna Cornelia; and David's eldest son was the fourth in four generations to have the name David Johannes du Plessis.
22. Du Plessis, *A Man Called Mr. Pentecost*, 53.

attention, and someone from the National Party of South Africa, the ruling party at the time, noticed him. Later that week, this man approached David with an invitation to get into politics, as he was certainly a capable orator and a passionate speaker. David was flattered, of course, and saw it as an opportunity to serve both God and country. However, after discussing the option with some of the other members of the Upper Room, most notably Mrs. J. B. M. Hertzog, the prime minister's wife, he recognized it for the distraction that it was and returned his focus to his ministry duties.

The second major temptation grew out of a commitment he had made in 1930, after he and Anna had been called out of Pretoria to the town of Bethlehem in the Orange Free State. David took over the mission newspaper he had started working for in 1920, *Comforter and Messenger of Hope*, which was failing. Through a special agreement, he moved the headquarters of the paper from Johannesburg to Bethlehem so that he could oversee it. David loved this work, and under his careful hand, the paper prospered.

However, it was the 1930s, and South Africa felt the Great Depression as severely as many other parts of the world. The press that printed the *Comforter* was owned and operated by the *Bethlehem Express*, and it looked as if it would soon go into bankruptcy because of poor management, not to mention the financial hard times everyone was experiencing. David ended up raising the capital necessary to purchase the paper by selling shares, and he made it profitable again through his shrewd management. This career seemed like another great opportunity for him to serve God and his community. However, he recognized that it was a distraction, as well, when his shareholders wanted to expand the paper and employ David full-time in its management, a position that would require him to give up his ministry work and devote all of his efforts to the paper. His decision boiled down to taking the job or resigning and leaving town, because of the many community leaders who would be angered if he declined their offer. With his wife's counsel, he did the latter, although he continued to serve as editor of the *Comforter.*

The same year that he took over the *Bethlehem Express,* David was ordained, at the age of twenty-five. In 1932, he finished second in the elections of the general secretary of the Apostolic Faith Mission (AFM) and won the post in 1936, a position he held until he resigned in 1947. As general secretary of the AFM, David was in charge of organizing the tour and scheduling speaking arrangements for Smith Wigglesworth, who came to the country the same year David was elected general secretary. At the time, David was still a young man of thirty.

Smith Wigglesworth Visits South Africa

Although David goes more deeply in his sermon into the events around this visit and how it led to Smith Wigglesworth's prophecy, which we will discuss in the next chapter, it bears mentioning briefly here. It is also worth discussing David's mind-set and future vision for his own ministry at the time. That God came to him roughly a decade and a half before this prophecy was to be fulfilled is also a sign of how much David needed to change before he could be the man God need him to be to help accomplish it.

When Smith Wigglesworth came to him, David no fan of the mainline denominational churches. His run-ins with the Dutch Reformed Church, which considered Pentecostals little better than heretics, greatly colored his opinions of traditional churches. His vision—like that of most, if not all, Pentecostals at the time—was that the baptism of the Holy Spirit would sweep true believers out of the denominations and into Pentecostal churches. Yet the essence of Smith Wigglesworth's prophecy to him was that he would take Pentecost to them, rather than the other way around. That this young man from South Africa would be chosen by God to come to the United States and be a major catalyst of the charismatic renewal in the traditional denominations is no less astounding. Yet this was just the case, and so it was that Smith Wigglesworth pinned this young man to the wall of his AFM office in 1936 and told him where God would lead him in the second half of the twentieth century.

At the General Council of the Assemblies of God in Memphis, Tennessee, 1937
Front row, left to right: Stanley H. Frodsham, C. A. Lasater, J. W. Welch, David du Plessis, E. S. Williams, J. Roswell Flower, and Archibald Cooper
Back row, left to right: E. L. Newby, J. Narver Gortner, W. I. Evens, D. N. Buntain, J. R. Evans, Noel Perkin, Donald Gee, and Howard Carter

In 1937, David was invited to address the General Counsel of the Assemblies of God in Memphis, Tennessee. This was not only his first trip to the United States; it was also his first trip outside of South Africa. This would be the first of many incremental steps that would push David into a position of world leadership among Pentecostals. It seemed that God wanted to teach him how to unify one group of believers before He sent him to address the larger issues of worldwide church reunification. One of the major issues he faced in getting the Pentecostals of South Africa to talk with one another was that of baptism. Some believed in baptizing by submersion three times—once in the name of the Father, again in the name of the Son, and a third time in the name of the Holy Spirit. However, others believed only one dunk was necessary. This was perhaps why David would later soar above such issues on the world stage as he emphasized "Christ, the baptizer in the Holy Spirit" in his teachings, to avoid issues that had traditionally divided other groups. Because his message was so different from anything they had heard before, it was a matter of accepting or rejecting it rather than splitting over different interpretations. While the war raged in Europe, David managed to promote the cause of Pentecostalism in South Africa, and while he was general secretary of the AFM, he helped start camp meetings and purchase a campground, established an orphanage, and oversaw the construction of new offices for the AFM. He also helped to start a Bible school and to reorganize the AFM constitution.

Left to right: Abolinus Schoeman of the Apostolic Faith Mission, H. B. Garlock, David du Plessis, and Edgar Pettenger in South Africa in 1947

At the war's end, David was also key to the organization of the first Pentecostal World Conference, which was held in Zurich, Switzerland, in May 1947. David ended up giving the keynote address for the conference, a message entitled, "Gather the Wheat—Burn the Chaff,"[23] about coming into the maturity Christ has for all of us.

23. See chapter 11 for the complete text of this address.

David during the 1950s

David's Worldwide Ministry Begins

God led David to minister around Europe for a while and then brought him to the United States. Then, at 4 AM in Los Angeles one day, God told him to resign as general secretary of the AFM and follow Him for the next steps of his ministry. In short order, David cabled his resignation. The next morning, at exactly 4 AM, the Lord woke him and told him to cable Anna and tell her to sell everything and follow him—to Switzerland! He was unsure how she would react; she had always said that he could travel as much as he wanted, but she would stay in South Africa. Just one week after sending the cable, he received a thick letter from Anna, which said that the Lord had spoken to her and told her she was to go wherever the He sent him. Because of the speed of the post from South Africa to the United States at the time, David knew that she had written and mailed this letter before receiving his telegram. Again, the Lord had prepared everything ahead of time.

They moved to Basel, Switzerland, where David continued to assist the leadership with the upcoming Pentecostal World Conference. While David was in Switzerland, he and his family received the news that Smith Wigglesworth had passed on. Yet, right to the end, the Apostle of Faith had held his conviction that David

While David was in Switzerland, he and his family received the news that Smith Wigglesworth had passed on. Yet, right to the end, the Apostle of Faith had held his conviction that David would do just as he had seen in the Lord's vision.

would do just as he had seen in the Lord's vision. In his last discussion with David, Smith had said, "My brother David, I've had no further word from the Lord. But I am absolutely sure that what He revealed in South Africa is coming and that you are the man for it."[24] Once Smith had passed, it was time for David to start watching for the prophecy to take place. David and his family didn't know what else to do except continue following the Lord as closely as they could, which turned out to be exactly the right course of action.

Disaster Leads to Revelation

The following year, while David traveled and ministered in the United States, he was involved in a major accident. He was traveling with Pastor Paul Walker in a 1958 Packard on a foggy West Virginia mountain road when their vehicle struck a train. David found himself hospitalized for a recovery that would last several months. Meanwhile, American Pentecostals gathered in Des Moines, Iowa, and formed the Pentecostal Fellowship of North America. The first course of action the group took was to gather an offering for David and his family that amounted to $400 and to promise to support them with $250 a month until he had fully recovered. With this money and some other offerings, David was able to send a thousand dollars to Anna with his request that she move their family to the United States. They were reunited in time to gather around David's hospital bed for Thanksgiving dinner.

24. Du Plessis, *A Man Called Mr. Pentecost*, 157.

While he was recovering, David had significant blocks of time to pray and seek the Lord. During this period, the Lord again spoke to him about Smith Wigglesworth's prophecy. He recorded the Lord's message in his autobiography as follows:

> "The time for the fulfillment of the prophecy Smith Wigglesworth gave you has arrived. It is time to begin. I want you to go to the leaders of the churches."
>
> I argued back, "Lord, what can I say to those dead churches?"
>
> "I can raise the dead." As simple as that.
>
> "But, Lord, they are enemies," I almost whined.
>
> "Yes, but I have told you to love your enemy."
>
> Ignoring the truth of Scripture in my frustration, I continued to argue. "How can I love people like this? I can agree with neither their doctrines nor their practices."
>
> "Well," the Lord said firmly, deep inside of me, "you will have to forgive them!"
>
> "Dear Lord"—it was just a whine by then—"how can I forgive them if I can't justify them?"
>
> "I never gave you authority to justify anybody. I only gave you authority to forgive. And if you forgive, you will love them. And if you love, you will want to forgive. Now you choose."[25]

When the conversation was over, David had seen his error.[26] He'd expected the Lord to bring him in like a prophet to pound the people with the truth, yet God was asking him to go to them in meekness and humility and to simply share. The revival would come through forgiveness offered without its being asked for.

25. Du Plessis, *A Man Called Mr. Pentecost*, 158.

26. See chapter 13—David's sermon entitled "Seventy Times Seven"—for more on his revelation of the importance of forgiveness.

While David wanted to come in like Jonah and prophesy doom over them unless they repented, he was to come in as a servant and offer the truth. It would be a revival birthed from forgiveness, not fight. It took some time for David to get his mind around this fact, and he spent a lot of time meditating on 1 Corinthians 13 during the remainder of his hospital stay. The rest of his recovery would involve both physical and spiritual healing, and David would be taught about loving others and forgiving them in several different ways. God was changing him from a prosecutor and a perfectionist into a defender and an intercessor. It was not his place to go in and convict but to ride in on forgiveness and mercy and present the truth of the gospel and the baptism of the Holy Spirit as lovingly as he could.

David also continued to work on the details of the 1949 Pentecostal World Conference (PWC) from his hospital room and later attended the meeting in Paris on his crutches. Here, armed with his more profound understanding of love and forgiveness, David was very effective in stopping the arguments so that the conference could go on in peace and growing unity. David pulled all the key leaders of opposing factions into what was to be an overnight meeting, and he quickly reconciled them. Because of this, the first order of the next day was approving their report and then agreeing that the Pentecostal World Conferences would continue regularly every third year. The next conference would be in London in 1952, and David would be the secretary. God was increasing David's grace to be a reconciler, first among the Pentecostals and then, eventually, with more traditional denominations.

In the meantime, David was offered a teaching position at Lee College in Cleveland, Tennessee, which gave the family a reason to stay in the United States, as well as provided support for them as they prepared for the London PWC. In 1952, David resigned his post at Lee College and moved his family to Stamford, Connecticut, where he served as interim pastor at an Assemblies of God church.

He also felt it was important to be away from Pentecostal centers of power—Springfield for the Assemblies, Cleveland for the Church of God, and so on—and closer to centers of the traditional denominations, namely, New York. Throughout this time, David continued to stay open to what he had been told through Smith Wigglesworth's vision, but, as of yet, he had not seen an open door to pursue it.

The Lord Opens the Door to the Ecumenicals

One day, as he was reading the newspaper, David came across a statement by Dr. John A. MacKay, president of Princeton Theological Seminary and a major Presbyterian leader. Previously, David had read that Dr. MacKay had called the Pentecostal missionaries in Latin and South America "the fly in the ointment of Protestantism." He had seen them as a hindrance to everything that the Protestants were trying to accomplish in these areas. Yet, in this article, Dr. MacKay said that the Pentecostal movement was the greatest blessing to the church in the twentieth century. David was curious about this apparent change of heart. Could this be his open door? He telephoned Dr. MacKay at Princeton and asked him about his quote. He found that Dr. MacKay had indeed experienced a change of heart regarding what the Pentecostals were doing, and he invited David to lunch. When David went to Princeton and met Dr. MacKay, "It was one of those rare and precious relationships in which both parties fully perceive the truth about the other—differences and all—and are in a twinkling of an eye united forever in the Spirit."[27] Their friendship would last for the rest of their lives.

A few days after this meeting, David felt prompted by the Spirit to visit the headquarters of the World Council of Churches in Manhattan. With little more than a nudge, he went and fumbled

27. Du Plessis, *A Man Called Mr. Pentecost*, 172.

while introducing himself to Dr. Roswell Barnes because he couldn't explain why he had come. However, Dr. Barnes and his staff were fascinated to have a Pentecostal in their midst, and David ended up spending the entire day with them, answering their questions and explaining Pentecostalism and the baptism in the Holy Spirit. It was just the divine introduction that David needed to reintroduce the traditional denominations to the Holy Spirit.

God was indeed at work, although it was not long before David felt the wrath of dogmatic Pentecostals for his decision to break boundaries that others wanted to remain intact.

God was indeed at work, although it was not long before David felt the wrath of dogmatic Pentecostals for his decision to break boundaries that others wanted to remain intact. However, for those listening to the Spirit instead of trying to please others, God's work was being done, just as Smith Wigglesworth had seen in his 1936 vision in South Africa. Not long after David's visit to the World Council, he received a call from Bill Wilson, the missions secretary for a group of smaller New England Pentecostal churches. He told David that the Lord had spoken to him about coming to David, because David would be able to help him with the problems their missions outreaches were having in Kenya and East Africa. The operations of their missions groups were extremely hindered by the government and traditional denominations in the area. David told him the only people he knew to contact were those he had met at the World Council, and David asked Bill if he could approach them on his behalf. Bill replied that all he knew was that God had told him David would have the answer, so he had come to him. Through his connections with Dr. MacKay and the World Council of Churches and the writing of a couple of letters, the matter was solved in the course of two months. God was working wonders, and David must have felt that he was just along for the ride.

When he contacted Dr. MacKay to thank him for his help, David was invited to attend the world conference for the International Missionary Council (IMC) in Germany, right on the heels of the 1952 PWC in London. David accepted, knowing he could easily extend his time for the PWC to attend the second event, but now he knew he was in the thick of it. The leading figures of the mainline denominations would be there, and he would be walking like Daniel into the mouth of a potential lions' den.

It just happened that Dr. MacKay was still president of the IMC, and when David walked in, Dr. MacKay greeted him quite warmly and introduced him to everyone there. David had planned on staying three days, but he ended up attending all eleven days of the conference and had 110 interviews among the 210 delegates. Their main question? "Okay, now," they would usually say, "start at the beginning and explain Pentecostalism to me."[28] From this meeting, people began to refer to David as "Mr. Pentecost."

As a result of his time at the IMC convention in 1952, David also received an invitation to attend the second assembly of the World Council of Churches (WCC), which was to take place in 1954 in Evanston, Illinois. In order for him to attend, he was asked to serve on the staff for the WCC and as a correspondent for the Far East Broadcasting Company, a company for which he had also worked during these years. It was here that David's message changed, from centering on Pentecost and the baptism in the Holy Spirit to Christ as the baptizer in the Holy Spirit. This shift seemed to make his message resonate with all who heard it, and he would retain this emphasis for the rest of his ecumenical ministry. As David said in his autobiography:

> Right this present day, I hardly ever minister without first giving a brief resume of my life, emphasizing the experience of forgiving "aught against any." This is the message

28. Du Plessis, *A Man Called Mr. Pentecost*, 177.

of Jesus—forgiving the Cross, imparting the Spirit, and directing us to continue that ministry of forgiveness. Then comes the baptism in the Holy Spirit. Then come the miracles.[29]

In 1956, David was invited to a retreat of ecumenical leaders in Connecticut. He was invited to speak candidly on the issues surrounding the Holy Spirit, the Pentecostal movement, and the growing charismatic renewal. David poured out his heart to those in attendance, and they still wanted more. David later remembered this as one of the greatest meetings of his life.[30] Soon after, David began to do what would have been unthinkable to him before hearing Smith Wigglesworth's prophecy—he began advising ministers who had received the baptism of the Holy Spirit to remain in their denominations rather than flee to the safety of Pentecostal churches. The charismatic renewal was in full swing!

Anna and David in 1972

At the same time, David was getting mixed reviews from his Pentecostal brethren. They were unsure of what he was doing, and in the absence of communications from him, many assumed the worst—that he was compromising the message and had backslidden. In 1955, he did not receive an invitation to the PWC in Stockholm—not that he had money to go, anyway—but when he offered his services to

29. Du Plessis, *A Man Called Mr. Pentecost*, 180.

30. David discussed this retreat in detail in the address that constitutes chapter 12 of this book.

them again in a letter, he was asked to be secretary for the 1958 conference, which was slated to be in Toronto. Even so, a strange coolness toward him grew. Not knowing what to think, and not having the courage or maturity to simply ask, others began to avoid him rather than deal openly with their reservations about him. Official discussions went on without David's knowledge. When he confronted one of the board members about it, he was told that he was seen as being too interested in—obsessed with, even—liberal, traditional denominations and independent Pentecostal churches. He just didn't fit like they wanted him to, so they systematically excluded him. The stronger, more established organizations seemed to be pushing out those that were smaller or peripheral. David was on a road for unity among the brethren and in the Spirit, but it seemed more and more like he was on it alone.

While doors seemed to be shutting on David within Pentecostalism, they were being swung wide open in the traditional denominations. In 1959, he spoke in places as varied as Princeton Seminary; the eighteenth council of the Presbyterian World Alliance in Sao Paulo, Brazil; the Ecumenical Institute of the World Council of Churches at Chateau de Bossey in Switzerland; and the Evangelical Congregational School of Theology in Myerstown, Pennsylvania; among others. He presented every audience with the straight facts of Pentecostalism and Jesus Christ, the baptizer in the Holy Spirit.

While doors seemed to be shutting on David within Pentecostalism, they were being swung wide open in the traditional denominations.

The Door Opens to the Catholic Church

A new breakthrough came when David spoke at a gathering in St. Andrews, Scotland, by invitation of the Commission on Faith and Order of the World Council of Churches. This was in preparation for the third assembly of the World Council of Churches, which was to meet in New Delhi in 1961.[31] The topic was "Jesus Christ, the Light of the World." David had his first encounter here with a Roman Catholic priest, Father Bernard Leeming, who just happened to be a personal friend of Pope John XXIII. Through this relationship, God would eventually open the door for David to minister in Rome and at the Vatican. David ministered there on the way back from the WCC New Delhi assembly, where his message was well received overall.

David with Pope Paul VI, who was pope from 1963–78

Despite this growing flow of the Spirit, in 1962, David received a letter saying that his papers as a minister with the Assemblies of God—credentials he had obtained shortly after moving to the United States—were being pulled. No reason was given, just notice that he was no longer ordained by their body.

David took this as a minor setback, however, and continued the work God had called him to and shown him through the vision given to Smith Wigglesworth. David had too much of the Lord's work to do to worry about who was ordaining him or not. While

31. David attended every WCC conference from 1956 until the end of his ministry, even though, after 1962, he had no official ties to or sponsorship of any denomination or church body.

the mainline Pentecostals were no longer calling him to speak at their meetings, the rest of the Christian world was.

While the 1950s seemed to be the crucial years of breakthrough for David, the 1960s and 1970s would be major years of spreading the gospel wherever doors were opened. He would average over 100,000 miles of travel each year, ministering to the broadest group of people imaginable. The du Plessis family changed homes a couple of times over these decades. When it appeared that Anna was suffering from the cold winters, they moved to Dallas, Texas, where David ended up working and traveling frequently with Gordon Lindsey of *The Voice of Healing*. Six years later, they moved to Oakland, California. These decades proved to be incredibly busy times. By then, David's work had been validated again in the eyes of most Pentecostals, although his credentials as a minister were not reinstated until 1979.

In 1972, as a result of the Vatican's desire to understand the growing Charismatic Renewal going on around the world in Catholic churches, David was crucial in initiating a series of dialogues between the Roman Catholic Church and a team of Pentecostals led first by himself and then, eventually, by his youngest brother, Justus. Because he did not belong to any of the formal Pentecostal denominations, he became the perfect man for the job, as there were strained relationships between mainline Pentecostal denominational churches and Catholic churches around the world, especially in South America. These dialogues spanned four- or five-year periods, continuing into the 1990s, but David served as the chairman of the Pentecostal side in the initial two, which spanned 1972–1976 and 1977–1982. It is easy to say that

David was crucial in initiating a series of dialogues between the Roman Catholic Church and a team of Pentecostals led first by himself and then, eventually, by his youngest brother, Justus.

these dialogues would never have happened except for the constant efforts of David and his counterpart on the Catholic side, Father Kilian McDonnell. Martin Robinson described David as "the chief architect"[32] of these talks and said he was instrumental to the tone and camaraderie of the discussions. At the end of the second set of dialogues, both David and Father McDonnell resigned and offered to serve as "chairmen emeritus" in order to make room for others to take part in the meetings. Another note about this incredible opening was that David himself ministered in St. Peter's Basilica as part of the 1975 Congress on Charismatic Renewal in the Catholic Church. The one frustration was that, despite the impact this had on the Catholic Church in paving the way for the Charismatic Catholic Movement, none of the Pentecostals in either the first world (such as executives from the Assemblies of God in the U.S.) or the third world (such as Pastor Paul Yonggi Cho of South Korea, who was also invited to attend) would be involved officially, despite the best efforts of both sides.

David and Anna greet Pope John Paul II.

David presenting a paper at the first round of Catholic-Pentecostal Dialogues in Rome

32. Robinson, "To the Ends of the Earth: The Pilgrimage of an Ecumenical Pentecostal, David J. du Plessis (1905–1987)," 233.

Years of Faithful Service Are Finally Recognized

David was recognized time and again for his work, having been the only significant leader to be part of the three most noteworthy Christian movements of the twentieth century: the Pentecostal movement, the charismatic renewal, and the ecumenical movement. In the September 9, 1974, issue of *Time* magazine, David was mentioned alongside such people as Billy Graham, Hans Küng, Jürgen Moltmann, and Rosemary Ruether, as one of the eleven greatest "shapers and shakers" of Christianity in the twentieth century. On May 23, 1976, St. John's University in Collegeville, Minnesota, presented him with the Pax Christi award. In May 1978, he finally received a D.D. that honestly gave him the title of "Dr. du Plessis" when Bethany Bible College in Santa Cruz, California, awarded him an honorary doctorate. As a result of these things and a growing acknowledgment that David had been following God throughout his ecumenical involvement, his Assemblies of God ordination papers were reissued in 1979. Then, on November 9, 1983, David was honored with the Benemerenti Medal by Pope John Paul II, an award for outstanding service to all of Christianity. It was the first time this award had been given by the Roman Catholic Church to someone who was not a Catholic.

At the invitation of Fuller Theological Seminary in Pasadena, California, David formally donated his personal papers and library to what would become the David du Plessis Archive, which still exists today. Then, from 1985 until his death, David also served at the seminary as their Resident Consultant for Ecumenical Affairs, with part of his duties being to organize this archive.

It is also worth noting here that one of the marks of David's integrity was that, while he could have profited greatly by this incredible outreach to the churches of the world, he never did. Time and again, David gave up what looked to be finally a financially stable situation and home for his family in order to uproot, relocate, and again face financial uncertainty as he followed the voice of God. From time to time, he would receive offers to join certain groups for large sums of money. He easily could have started his own denomination, from those who flocked to him for advice, but he never did. He encouraged the ministers who came to him to remain in their denominations, and he refused to ever market or exploit his message for his own popularity or wealth.

David's final days came when, during a routine gall bladder operation in August 1986, the doctors discovered David had inoperable abdominal cancer. David passed away within a few months, on February 2, 1987, just five days short of his eighty-second birthday.

3

"The Wigglesworth Prophecy": A Sermon by David du Plessis

(Note: Rev. David du Plessis gave this sermon in 1970. It is the only remaining recording of Dr. du Plessis speaking on the prophecy given to him by Smith Wigglesworth.)[33]

In 1936, I was still a young man—only thirty years—and secretary of the largest Pentecostal organization in South Africa. It was started when two Americans came—John Lake and Tom Hezmalhalch—in 1908. They began their meetings in Johannesburg, with the old Zion people—Doweyites,[34] some used to call them.

Zion had healings, divine healing. Dowie was very wonderful, but he saw the baptism of the Holy Spirit quite differently than we did. Yet the elders in this early movement were men and women from Zion who had received the baptism, and other Zion people followed them. They came together in that old Presbyterian church that could seat about six hundred and had eighteen months of revival that went on every night of the year. During that time, there never was a night without a meeting. Weekend services usually began Friday night, went all through the night, all through Saturday, all through Saturday night, all through Sunday until midnight, and then everyone would

33. The transcription of this sermon has been edited to improve the clarity.
34. "Doweyites": Those following the ministry of John Alexander Dowie.

go and get some sleep before they went to work on Monday morning. Every weekend, there were miracles and more miracles.

This movement grew among both the white and black throughout the country. In 1932, I became the general secretary of what was known as the Apostolic Faith Mission (the AFM). It was during my time as secretary of the AFM that Reverend Smith Wigglesworth came to visit us and speak throughout South Africa. It was wonderful to hear all the wonderful things God did through him, even though he was not a greatly educated, learned theologian but was just a simple believer. In fact, Reverend Wigglesworth never wrote a line in his whole life; he could only sign his name. His wife had taught him how to do that.

He had never learned to read, he had never been to school, and he started working as a plumber when he was a young boy. When he came to the Lord, he wanted to read the New Testament, so he sat and tried to read it with the help of his wife, and then one day, all of a sudden, it made sense to him—he could read the New Testament. He said that God had taught him how.

Now, I have met others who have experienced similar things—I knew a Russian woman here in America who couldn't read English, and the Lord taught her how to read English. She could read Russian before, but Brother Wigglesworth had never read before.

And so, when I met him, he told me that he never, ever reads anything but the Word of God—no pamphlets, nothing but the New Testament. And he said, "I think I know the New Testament from Matthew to Revelation, and I can quote it and wouldn't even make a mistake in the punctuation." He had memorized the entire New Testament. If you asked him to, he could quote chapter after chapter of it to you.

When he came to South Africa, he had wonderful meetings. Because I arranged all of his meetings throughout the country as

General Secretary and attended all of them, we became very close friends. Then, when he came to Johannesburg to work in that area—the area we call the Rand, where roughly three million people live around and between, from Johannesburg center to Pretoria center, in an area of about fifty square miles—we decided he should stay with us in our home. We had a reasonably large home, not because we had such a large family, but my wife found it convenient to always keep some help with us so we had time and energy to keep the faith fight going. We didn't have boarders, and we had lots of room.

When he came, my wife was a little worried about this strange old gentleman, because if you ever saw him in action, he was a sight to behold. I have seen people try to imitate other ministers in their style, but I have never seen anyone ever try to imitate Brother Wigglesworth. The truth is, there is really no way anyone ever could! What's more, if he couldn't find a word, he made one up, but somehow everyone understood what he meant. What he liked about me was that I always understood him, and so I made a good interpreter for him. He would preach English, and I'd interpret into Afrikaans.

He stayed with us, and we found him to be the finest old gentleman to entertain. He didn't eat very much, and he always told me just what he wanted to eat. He was very nice about it. He always finished quickly, and then he'd say, "Well, you can't only feed your body. Now it is time to also feed our souls." Then he would start quoting Scripture right at the table, before you'd even finished your meal or served the dessert. He was really splendid that way, the way he emphasized God's Word in everything.

One day he said to me, "Brother, if anybody can ever catch me without a New Testament on my body, I'll give him five pounds sterling."

I said, "You always have a New Testament on your body?"

He said, "Yes."

I said, "How about when you take a shower?"

He said, "Then I lock the door." In other words, I would never catch him without a Bible in his pocket.

He carried a proper New Testament that was nice and flat. I liked it so much that I decided someday I'd get one like it—now I think I've got a half a dozen of them. He always had a New Testament like that, he always spoke from it, and he believed every word of it that he spoke. He was really an apostle of faith—the same very simple faith he always preached. There is a book of his sermons called *Ever Increasing Faith* that I think everyone should read because it will increase your faith. If you ever find a copy, buy it and read it cover to cover.

Brother Wigglesworth was a wonderful evangelist with a mighty healing ministry. I must say, I've been with healers since then—I have seen Brother Branham in action and even traveled with him for a while, I've seen the Jeffreyses in England in action among others, and I have also seen Tommy Osborn and Tommy Hicks, as well as many others. For a while, I worked with the *Voice of Healing*, and, through that experience, I met some seventy healing evangelists—good, bad, and indifferent, all kinds. I know all about it, but not one have I ever seen that had the ministry that Smith Wigglesworth had. Everybody in South Africa was interested in this strange old gentleman who knew so much, even though he had learned so little from the world. His gospel was unadulterated. He never quoted what anybody else said—because he never read what anybody said. He only quoted what God said in His Word. It's a temptation to quote these other things, you know—we need to keep the Word of God first place in such things.

Early one morning around six o'clock, he walked into our kitchen unannounced while my wife, Anna, was busy cooking breakfast. He stepped in and asked, "Where's David?" She replied, "Brother Wigglesworth, he's gone to the office already." You see, I used to get up at five, and then get ready, and by six o'clock I'd be in my office. Then, from six to nine, I would dictate all of my letters so that when the girls came in at nine o'clock, they'd have everything recorded, and they could go on with their work, and I could start my counseling sessions and consultations and other appointments. That's the way I've pretty much always regulated my life.

So, I was at the office. When Brother Wigglesworth heard this, he turned around and shouted down the passage to his son-in-law, Jimmy Salter, "Jimmy!" and Jimmy woke up and came out and said, "Yes, Dad? What's wrong?"

"Where's Compton?" Compton, one of our workers, was driving for them.

Jimmy said, "Oh, he's still asleep."

He said, "Wake him up—I must see David at once." Jimmy did, and in a little while the car left. It was twelve miles from our home to my office.

Alice Salter (Smith's eldest daughter) and her husband, James "Jimmy" Salter

All I remember of it was that I was sitting quietly, working at my desk, when suddenly the door flew open. I hadn't even heard any footsteps! All I knew was that, all of a sudden, that door flew open almost with a bang, and there stood Brother Wigglesworth. He walked forward, stood up straight, and commanded me, "Get up from there! Come out here!"

I stood up and immediately came over to him. He put his hands on my shoulders and pushed me up against the wall, looked straight in my eyes, and began to prophesy. I'll never forget the first words of what he said: "The Lord says, 'You have been in your Jerusalem long enough. You have to go to the uttermost parts of the earth, and He is going to send you.'"

I'll never forget the first words of what he said: "The Lord says, 'You have been in your Jerusalem long enough. You have to go to the uttermost parts of the earth, and He is going to send you.'"

There are a lot of things the Lord will say to you now, as if it has already happened or already exists, but, from our time frame, it is only that He intends to make it so. Brother Wigglesworth began to prophesy to me some things I knew, some that I didn't believe, some that I didn't want, and some I didn't expect to get or thought were completely out of my reach and out of my field—things that were outside of my own personal vision for my future. I had a vision that the Pentecostal movement would sweep the earth, but I thought it would pull people out of the old mainline churches, or at least that it would be a movement separate from those churches, forming a new church. But that is not what Brother Smith was telling me. He began to prophesy that I would travel more than most men traveled in their lives. He said, "And you will have the privilege to see and to participate in the most glorious and mightiest sweeping revival that has ever been known in Christian history. It will come through the old-line denominations"—that's what he called them. We call them now the traditional denominations or historic churches; they call us classic Pentecostals. We are classic already, we're so old. We need renewal as well.

He continued to prophesy, "It is coming in a remarkable way. Ministers will accept the truth and accept the baptism, and the churches will begin to accept this glorious enduement [or gift]." As he prophesied, he made no distinctions between any of the churches, and I thought, *Well, we haven't got anything like what he is talking about, even among the Pentecostals. This is a totally new level of revival. We've been praying for something like this, but we want it for ourselves to show everyone else how special we are—we don't really want it for everyone as he is describing now.*

In fact, he actually said that it would come through the other groups, not our own, and that I would have a part in it. He went on describing it until he finally said, "It's no use. I can't tell you any more, because there are some things that even I don't understand, and I don't know how to explain them to you. I am telling you these." Later I learned that he had seen visions of this revival that God was sending between two o'clock and four that morning.

After he had prophesied and unburdened his heart, he just bowed his head and said, "Lord, bless him." Then he turned, walked out, and closed the door.

I stood there for a moment, wondering why he hadn't discussed the vision with me, but finally I returned to my desk and sat back down, leaned my head on my hands, and began to pray, "Lord, I accept the warning about the revival to come, but if this is going to happen, I will need to be guided by You very, very clearly. No matter who the messenger is, I cannot go by what others say." Woe be to anyone who lets their life be directed by some prophet or prophetess without confirming that word with the Spirit that lives within them as well.

The Guide—the Holy Spirit—lives within us, and because He dwells in us, New Testament prophecy is not like Old Testament prophecy. In the Old Testament, the Spirit moved *upon* the prophet to speak to the people, but there was no Spirit *in* the people, so they just had to listen to the words of the prophet and obey. But today, the church is a body born of the Spirit, and the Spirit is in each of us. You can't talk to us as if we were people who don't know the Spirit. That's why every one of us has to know how to be led by the Lord for ourselves. It is our responsibility. We have to know when it is the Spirit of God speaking to us and when it is an imposter.

In the end, I don't know how long I sat there at my desk, puzzling over what had just happened, but a gentle knock at the door woke me out of my thoughts. "Come in," I said. When the door opened, there stood Smith Wigglesworth again.

"Good morning, Brother David," he greeted me, as if it was the first time he'd seen me that morning. The first time he'd entered, he didn't greet me at all, just ordered me, "Come out of there!" He didn't ask how I was or anything like that—in fact, he wasn't even gentle. Yet this time, he was very gentle. After he greeted me, he asked, "How are you?"

I answered, "Well, Brother Wigglesworth, greatly puzzled."

He said, "Why?"

I said, "Because you have been in here, you talked to me, you prophesied, you told me visions, and now you come in and greet me as if you never saw me."

He said, "The Bible says, 'The Lord said to the prophet, "Greet no man on the way."'"

"Yes," I said.

"Well, I didn't greet your wife, I didn't greet Salter, I didn't greet Compton, I didn't greet you, until I delivered the message. But now the prophet has delivered the message, and that's why I've come back to discuss it with you. What do you think of it?"

I said, "Brother Wigglesworth, I am really amazed, and I just want to ask you, have you got Scripture for such a thing?" I always like to ask for Scripture, because when I can say it is written, then I can have faith.

He said, "Yes, I have Scripture. The Lord told me what Scripture to give you: Acts 6 and 7. 'The Word of God increased and the number of disciples multiplied in Jerusalem greatly.' That's the description of the first Pentecostal church at the beginning of the church. And then afterwards, after the church had so flourished, a great company of priests were obedient to the faith." And he said, "This is what the Lord wants me to explain to you.

"First, it's a layman's movement—a fisherman's movement. But the second wave that comes becomes a clergy/priesthood movement. And after the work had been thoroughly established by the Holy Spirit in the laity and God had proved Himself, then some priests will come in, and there will be a great, tremendous move because of the priests."

After he had explained this further, he said to me, "I wish I was younger, for according to what the Lord said to me, you will see this great change. This great move of the Spirit will come round about the middle of the century"—that would be about fifteen years after we were speaking that morning in 1936—"then you will see it."

Well, the Lord warned me plenty of time in advance, didn't He? Fifteen years—and I have never forgotten. He said then, "Also remember this: you don't have to worry about doing anything at all, or seeing much of it, until I have gone home. For the Lord made it very clear to me that I must not preach this, and I must not attempt to stop anything. I must leave it alone. He will work it out, but it will not even begin while I'm alive, so I won't even see the beginnings of it. That's why I wish I was twenty years younger, so that I could see these beginnings, but you will see them."

Then he said, "Now a word of warning: God says all the things that I have told you will come to pass, and you will see them, and you will have a part in them, with only these conditions: that you remain humble and faithful. If you can remember those two things—remain humble and faithful—then God will use you in a way that no one else is used, an unusual way. It will not be the trend—it will be you and God—but you must stay humble and remain faithful."

I have never apologized for Pentecost—that's why they call me "Mr. Pentecost." I refuse to be anything but Pentecostal. I'm not Protestant, I'm not evangelical, I'm not a fundamentalist—I'm all that plus Pentecost.

I can see today, if you're blessed and succeed, then there is the danger of getting puffed up and being proud of your achievements. Even if you have been faithful for a long time, there is still the danger that you may compromise. However, I am happy to say that I haven't yet found a Pentecostal brother that came to hear what I have taught at any ecumenical meeting that did not admit that I was not compromising. I have never apologized for Pentecost—that's why they call me "Mr. Pentecost." I refuse to be anything but Pentecostal. I'm not Protestant, I'm not evangelical, I'm not a fundamentalist—I'm all that plus Pentecost. Don't ever stop at being a fundamentalist. Don't ever stop being an evangelical. But there is more, always more.

I learned this from a man that some might not think was even such a dedicated Christian, but I knew him as a very dedicated Christian. Karl Barth[35] said to me, "The biggest mistake you could ever make was to think you've arrived, and stop going on." He said, "Jesus said, 'I am the way, I am the truth, and I am the life.' He is a way without a terminal. There is no end. You'll never arrive at

35. Karl Barth (1886–1968) was a Swiss Reformed theologian who taught in Germany and opposed Adolf Hitler before World War II. He was a founder of the Confessing Church and was best known for his move back to Scripture as the basis of religion rather than culture, science, psychology, or anything else. This concept was called neo-orthodoxy.

the end—until you're in glory, and that's not even the end yet." He went on to say, "And as you move on in the way, the truth will dawn on you. You can't see the truth now that you will see as you move further on along the way, any more than you can see what's beyond the hills. As the truth dawns on you, the light grows brighter and brighter. You will think that you can stop, but you've got to keep going."

As I was still pondering what Brother Wigglesworth had prophesied, he said to me, "Have you ever been airsick?"

I said, "Sir, I've never been in the air."

He says, "Do you get seasick?"

I said, "I've never been on the sea. I've never traveled outside of South Africa." I had been up and down, crisscross that country, and I knew every town and city in my country. I knew every Pentecostal work, movement, mission, and so on, but I'd never been out on the sea and I'd never been in the air. In those days, flying wasn't so common.

He said, "Well, you're going to fly a lot, and you will travel—more than most men, and you must not get sick. Come here!" Out I came again. He pushed me up against the wall, and now I think he finished his job—he prayed that I would never get sick when I traveled for the Lord. He told the Lord, he said, "Lord, You know it's awful to be sick at home, but it's ten times worse to be sick away from home, so don't let him ever get sick when he's working or traveling for You."

And, thank the Lord, I am not sick—I'm always well when I travel. If I'm tired at all, I get traveling again so that I can feel better. And I work hard at home. When I'm traveling, I don't have to work so hard, because I get a little more time to relax, but when I'm home, I work against time writing correspondence. In addition to that, I have lately turned my hand back to doing carpentry, which I haven't done for years, but it's good exercise. My Lord was a carpenter, you know. At the carpenter's bench down in my office, my wife put a little picture of Jesus working in the carpenter shop, and when I work around there, I'm still working for Him. It all reminds me of Him—wonderful Jesus.

After this, I didn't see Brother Wigglesworth again but a small handful of times. When he left the Rand area, he went down to Cape Town for meetings. I eventually followed him to Cape Town to help some big meetings, and right before I left for Cape Town, I got a letter from J. Roswell Flower, the General Secretary of the Assemblies of God, who passed on to be with the Lord July 23, just a few days ago.[36] He was 82. I received a lovely letter from him, inviting me to come to the United States in 1937 to be one of the speakers at the General Council of the Assemblies of God in Memphis, Tennessee.

So I came over in 1937 and then returned by way of England in 1938. There I met Brother Wigglesworth again, and I stayed with him at 70 Victor Road in Bradford. He had lived in 70 Victor Road from the day he got married. His wife passed away in that house; his daughter, Mrs. Salter, passed away in that house; and if Jimmy is still alive, he'll pass away in that house. Seventy Victor Road—that's where I met him.

Things were beginning to happen in Europe at that time. It looked like war, and, sure enough, I found soldiers everywhere in Europe, so I soon made for home. I didn't want to be in Europe when trouble hit—it was Hitler's days, and everybody was saying, "Stalin, Hitler, Mussolini, that's the great triumvirate[37]—that's the devil's crowd—and Pope Pius." Oh brother, you should have heard them preach—why, according to them, the Lord was coming in a few years' time.

36. This was in 1970.

37. "A group of three men jointly governing a realm." (William Morris, (ed.) *The American Heritage Dictionary of the English Language* [Boston: Houghton Mifflin Company, 1980], s.v., "triumvirate.")

So I went home and waited. The Second World War came. The Second World War carried on and then finally ended, and in 1947, we had our first Pentecostal World Conference. Sometime shortly after that, I stopped in again to see Brother Wigglesworth. It must have been late 1947 or in 1948. I had some meetings with him in England then, and again we discussed what he had told me in 1936, and again he told me some of the miracles he had seen in the vision, but I still could not really get enthused about it.

You see, the whole thing was not according to my own plans. To me, the Pentecostal World Conference seemed to be God's answer. Now that the Pentecostals were finally getting together, something was really going to happen, and we'd bury the dead old mainline churches. That was how I saw it at the time. Brother Wigglesworth said, "No, that's not it, the revival will come through the old line denominations. I don't know how you'll get in to reach them, but you'll get there. The Lord knows how." He wasn't worried.

In 1947, he died. In 1950, I made my first contacts with the historic churches. It was probably just the Lord leading me. Dr. John MacKay, who was president of the International Missionary Council, president of the United Presbyterian Church, and president of Princeton Seminary, said in a speech in New York, "The greatest blessing that has come to Christianity in this century is the Pentecostal movement."

I thought, *That's something for MacKay to say,* because when he worked in South America, he had said, "The Protestant work in South America is going on fine, except for the fly in the ointment"—and the fly was the Pentecostals. And you know what a fly does to the druggist's ointment? It makes it stink! This was the term he had used for the Pentecostals. Then he had said that the Pentecostals in South America were a fly in the ointment; now he was saying it was the greatest blessing that had come to the church in this century. So I called him to ask about this change of opinion.

By this time, I was Secretary of the Pentecostal World Conference and busy working on the London conference that would be held in 1952. I asked, "Dr. MacKay, could I meet you somewhere?" He said, "Come to Princeton and have lunch with me." When I told him who I was, he said, "Yes, I've heard of you—and I'd like to talk to you. You come along."

So I went to Princeton and had lunch with him and then spent the afternoon with him. That was the beginning of my coming into what we now call the ecumenical movement. He told me that when he had gone back to South America and seen what the Holy Spirit had done there and the Latin American countries, he concluded that if he had to make a choice between the uncouth life of the Pentecostals there and the certain death of the old formal churches, he would rather have the uncouth life of the Pentecostals.

I said, "That's wonderful."

He said, "Don't ever compromise or minimize your Pentecostal life and experience. God has established this movement." And we became fast friends.

At the time, I thought that was all there was to it, so I waited for God to make the next move. One day, Bill Wilson, whom some of you might know as the Mission Secretary for the Eastern Churches, came to my home and said, "David, the Lord has sent me through a word of prophecy that came last night in East Providence, Rhode Island. We have trouble with missionaries out on the African East Coast. The mainline denominational missions are blocking and hindering our work out there. When I prayed for a solution last night, the Lord said you can find the way to solve this problem."

I couldn't understand the Lord sending him to me. I said, "Why don't you try your evangelical contacts?"

"Try them! They rejected us. The Lord says you've got the solution."

I said, "Bill, the only solution I can think of is to talk with Dr. MacKay—he's the president of the International Missionary Council—and then perhaps he can help us in some way, and we can do something."

He said, "David, I don't know what the Lord knows that you can do, but the Lord knows you've got something you can do."

I said, "All right. Do you mind if I call on the World Council of Churches?"

"No."

I told my wife, "I am going to New York. I have contacted Dr. MacKay, and he has made an appointment for me in New York, and I'm going to New York to talk to the World Council people."

She said, "What are you going to say to them?"

I said, "I don't know; I'll see when I get there."

She said, "Well, I listened to you! All my life you've preached against these councils. Now what are you going to say?"

I said, "I might have to apologize—I might have to apologize." Oh, I was as faithful as you could find a man, but if I could, how I enjoyed reading stuff that makes these other groups and traditional denominations look bad, because I wanted them to be bad. We were the good guys; they were the bad guys. I only read the worst stuff about the Catholics, because I wanted to have an excuse to have nothing to do with them. It is easy to find an excuse to believe that the old crowd's too bad to associate with, that God is calling us to "come out from among them." Yet, if they were really as bad as we think, then we ought to go in and save them, not sit back and condemn them. Shouldn't we save bad people? Or are we only looking for good people to save? If you are looking for good people, you're looking for the other fellow's sheep, and I guarantee you'll end up with his goats. We are not called to sheep stealing; we are called to seek and save the lost.

After I decided to go, I remember praying, "Lord, You've told me to go to these people, and now this issue with Brother Wilson and the Pentecostal Missions is really giving me a good reason." So I went to New York.

When I arrived and was with them, I began to tell them about our Pentecostal missions. Of course, I had to talk about missions, since I had this situation in Kenya. Our brethren there were having difficulty because they couldn't get recognition from the Council of Churches, and the government therefore was cool on them. However, when I finished talking about the missions, the chief in the office there asked me to keep on telling him about Pentecost. When lunch came, there was finally a lull of silence. I said, "It's twelve o'clock and it's lunchtime. I'm sorry I took so much of your time."

He said, "No, you didn't take my time. I took yours, because I'm asking the questions." He asked, "You eat lunch?"

I said, "Yes."

He said, "I'll pay for it if you keep talking."

So we went to lunch, and I kept talking. When we came back, he called the office staff together, and he made me repeat to them all those things that I thought they didn't want to hear. I was sure he'd tell me to get out, but instead he kept me there. In the end, he asked me, "Where have you been all this time?"

I said, "Sir, I've only lived in America for a while. I'm a South African."

"Well, where are your Pentecostal leaders? None of them have ever come and talked to us. We can't get anyone from any Pentecostal group, anywhere, to come talk with us. How are we supposed to get ahold of these people when they always run away from us?"

I said, "Well, you call us Pentecostals 'crazy fanatics'—who wants to talk to a man that calls you a 'crazy fanatic'?"

"Yes," he said, "it may be true, but you call us 'unbelieving devils.'"

Now I said, "That's true, too, but I didn't come here to call you names."

He said, "That's why I'm not calling you names. I love to hear what you have to say. We've been waiting for a man like you."

In the end, I stayed there until four o'clock in the afternoon. When we finally finished, they asked me to write a letter to them recommending and endorsing the Pentecostal missions groups in East Africa—if I remember correctly, it was the Eagle Missionary Assemblies and some other group in Pennsylvania, and then Mrs. Gibson's people from the East Coast Zion Bible Institute. There were three groups, and I recommended and endorsed all of them. I said, "These are my brethren, and I know them to be honest, trustworthy men, and I would recommend that they get some protection or some help."

The office in New York wrote to the London office of the International Missionary Council—later on, I got acquainted with those secretaries—and they wrote to the British Colonial office in Kenya. In those days, Kenya and those eastern countries were still under British control. Not long afterwards, I learned that the British Colonial office had ordered their heads in the colonies to let these Pentecostal missions groups operate freely. Thank God for what's happened in East Africa since then.

That was the beginning of my cooperation with the ecumenical groups. They saw themselves as service groups. They said, "We are not here to control; we are here to serve." I wish every service agency that was ever established would remain a service agency, but God have mercy when service agencies become controlling agencies. That's where the trouble starts—when such groups begin to strive to control instead of serve.

I think for the rest, you know the story. In England, Brother Wigglesworth only told a few brethren that he knew there was a great revival coming. Something I left out was that, when I came here in 1937, I met Dr. Charles Price[38] in Pasadena, and we spent an afternoon together. He wanted to know all about Brother Wigglesworth. They had met, and they knew each other, but Dr. Price was a highly educated man, and Wigglesworth was an uneducated man. When they had met, Brother Wigglesworth would say, "I wish I could be like Charles Price," and Charles Price said to me, "I wish I had no education, and I was like Wigglesworth. Then I'd be more spiritual."

I told him then, "Brother Wigglesworth predicts that there is a tremendous revival that is going to sweep the world. The world—not some countries—but the world! And all the churches."

I told him then, "Brother Wigglesworth predicts that there is a tremendous revival that is going to sweep the world. The world—not some countries—but the world! And all the churches."

Dear old Charles Price just burst out in tears. "Oh," he said, "thank God, thank God. There's someone else who got the vision."

I said, "You got it, too?"

He said, "Yes, but I dare not talk about it. The brethren all say to me, in the last days the love of many shall wax cold. They believe that there will be no greater revival—that we Pentecostals are the last wave."

The last wave. No wonder I once heard a Pentecostal pastor say, "God has made us the holders of the Holy Spirit—if people want Him, let them come to *us*."

38. Dr. Charles S. Price (1887–1947) was a great Pentecostal leader in the United States during the first half of the twentieth century who moved greatly in the gifts of healings and miracles.

How sad. You know, when I think of this, I think the Catholic Church must have been Pentecostal at some point, because when Pentecostals begin to think they are *the* church, they're just like Catholics. "Now *we* are *the* church."

I remember the battle we had in the Church of God in Cleveland, Tennessee. You know, they used to be *the* Church of God, and nobody else but they were right. There are still some of them that believe that way. Well, thank God for shaking us up—and shaking us out of the old ruts that we've gotten ourselves into.

But my point is that Dr. Price confirmed all that Brother Wigglesworth had said to me, and these two old pioneers blessed me and encouraged me so much. So, friends, gradually I've come to move easily within different church circles. It began with missions work and at the World Council of Churches headquarters, and then, in 1952, they invited me to the International Missionary Council in Germany. It was there that Dr. MacKay did something very unusual. At such conferences, they never asked visitors to speak. They usually already have a program lined up well in advance. However, one day, a Methodist missionary was telling how our mainline Christian institutions were ruining Christianity in India. Years ago, revival had hit there, and the Methodist church established a school, but today that school has only 10 percent Christian students and only 5 percent Christian teachers, even though it's still a Methodist school. He said, "The best thing that could happen to us there is that someone set fire to the place and burn it down."

At that, Dr. MacKay got up, and he said, "All right, while you fellows are burning down your institutions, I want a gentleman that's with us here to come and tell us how the Pentecostals, without institutions, have been sweeping around the world with a missionary message that is shaking the earth." In those days—that's 1952—Pentecostals weren't as strong on education as we are today. Today, you can find a doctor on every Pentecostal platform. I don't know where they get these degrees, but some of them have no more warmth than the number of degrees they have. But, back in 1952, we Pentecostals didn't think too much of such degrees. However, the same was not true among ecumenicals, so when Dr. MacKay introduced me, he called me "*Dr.* du Plessis." Somehow, after that, it stuck. After that, people kept asking me, "Where did you get your doctorate?" To that, I would always answer, "I don't have one. It was just that Dr. MacKay called me 'Doctor' at a conference once and it stuck."

"I see," they'd say. "So, you haven't got a D.D.?"

"Oh, yes, I have a D.D., a small d.d.—it stands for 'David the Donkey.'"[39] That is what I had thought in 1920 when I began to work for the Lord: "I'm the Lord's Donkey." You see, David the Donkey was my title in South Africa. People still know me by that name if you're ever in South Africa.

Well, at that missionary conference, I saw where the churches were going. They asked me, "How did the Pentecostals do it?" I said, "By everyone being a witness. Each one teach one, witnessing, being Christians, living the life." Today, we're not about just being Christians but all about degrees. When churches call to find pastors, they want to know the man's educational qualifications. Missionaries have to have certain qualifications or they can't pass certain board requirements. They even make them take psychological tests. Good Lord, have mercy upon us if an ungodly psychiatrist has to make the judgment of the fitness of a Spirit-filled man and woman for the missions field—for how could he understand? Where does

Missionaries have to have certain qualifications or they can't pass certain board requirements. They want clever people, but it's the foolishness of the gospel that has changed these countries, not the wisdom of men.

39. David did, however, earn his own D.D. in 1978 from Bethany Bible College in Santa Cruz, California, as recognition of his life's work and teachings.

he get his information? Is he getting it from ungodly psychiatrists in other countries? None of us can fit into that kind of man-devised frame, because "the natural man receiveth not the things of the Spirit."[40] They are forever foolishness to him, and they don't want to send fools out to these foreign countries. They want clever people, but it's the foolishness of the gospel that has changed these countries, not the wisdom of men.

So today, the Lord has changed things to the point that I can hardly believe it sometimes. I am so at ease—and so happy—in all kinds of meetings, but thank God for the men and brethren that have been willing to help me in this. Once, I was supposed to go to an institute in New York and I couldn't go, so I asked Brother Spencer to go for me. Here and there, I have found brethren who are willing to go. In some cases, I've recommended Pentecostal leaders willing to go and speak at certain conferences. Yet, when they received the invitation, they absolutely refused to go.

But I never refused. I've gone if I can, even though sometimes I can't for financial reasons. Believe me, there isn't money in this kind of an outreach. If I wanted to make money, I should try to be an evangelist or something like that—you know, spend an hour raising an offering and then preach for half an hour. But I didn't go that way. However, I do believe the Lord still honors faith and obedience, and so He takes care of me.

Recently this year, I had to go to Indonesia, and I wasn't sure if God wanted me to go. Then a brother knocked at my door, came in, sat down, and shared a few wonderful Scriptures with me. When he finished, I said, "This is just what I needed to encourage me on my way to Indonesia."

"Oh yes," he said, "but the Lord also told me to give you this," and he handed me a thousand dollars. So, that takes care of it. Not only the promises, but also the blessing with it.

---

40. 1 Corinthians 2:14.

When I had to go to Chile, just last May, I had only two days to speak at a conference of four hundred ministers. I prayed, "Lord, I haven't got time to stay longer."

He said, "Go."

I said, "Lord, the fare is $770. You want me to spend that much for only two days?"

"I'll pay your fare."

I had a meeting in Glendale at Faith Center that Sunday morning. They had already taken up all of the offerings for the day when the pastor said, "I feel we ought to help Brother David. He's got a call to Santiago, Chile." So they took up another offering. That evening he came and gave me a check for $600—my, that was great. He said, "That's not all," and he gave me another check for $170. Together they were $770! Exactly the fare I needed for the trip.

I said, "All right, Lord. If You pay that easily, I'll travel easy," and I went. Oh, what a time I had those three days in Chile—how the Lord blessed that trip! That's the way He takes care of things. That's the way He supplies.

Tomorrow, I will preach in the Episcopal church in Selma. On Monday, I will meet the ministers, and then we will go for a few days to a camp meeting in the mountains. Then we fly to Europe. When I was in London, England, last November, the Catholics invited Brother Ray Bringham and me to a conference in Spain. The cardinal said, "Will both of you come to a Pentecostal Charismatic Catholic conference at the university in Salamanca in Spain? The invitation is with the approval of the bishop!" So we're going to have a Pentecostal conference in Spain at a Catholic university.

From there, I will be making my first renewal visit with the Vatican in Rome—not with the pope, though. I will meet with the cardinal who is president of the Secretariat for Promoting Christian Unity, Cardinal Willebrands, and they have agreed they would now like to have dialogue with Pentecostals on September 2 and 3. So I'm going to Rome to meet with them.

Now, I know a Catholic priest who has said, "David is going to talk to the pope." I can only say, "Then that must be prophetic," because I haven't made such arrangements. However, if it happens when I get there, that would be all right. Will you pray that the Lord will help me? I have been in the Pentecostal movement now for the last fifty-two years—I received the baptism in 1918—and, my brethren, nowhere has this revival of the Holy Spirit sparked and moved as fast as it's now moving in Catholic churches. Not even in the original Pentecostal movements nor in the Protestant churches has the baptism of the Holy Spirit been received so quickly by so many.

The Spirit is moving throughout the world, and everywhere I go, I find people telling me how the Catholic priests and nuns and professors are embracing it. It really is a movement among the learned and the priests—among their educated and cultured people. Throw away those with other prophecies and all the naysayers—this revival, birthed by the Holy Spirit, is coming through, and the best of it still hasn't happened yet.

4

The Wigglesworth Prophecy—Other Sources and Information

One of the problems in researching the Smith Wigglesworth prophecy to David du Plessis is finding the exact wording of what was said on that morning in December 1936. One of the main reasons for this is, of course, that it was never recorded or written down until sometime in the early 1950s. The earliest reference to it in the writings of David du Plessis is an article that was published in 1951:

> How well I remember the increased desire for fellowship when the late Smith Wigglesworth visited South Africa in 1936. One morning early he came into my office and without a word of greeting said: "Young man, you have been in Jerusalem long enough and the Lord says that you have to go to the uttermost parts of the earth." I was dumbfounded. "He has much work for you and you will be going soon." Then he prayed: "Lord, let him always enjoy Your blessings and never get sick on his many travels ahead." Later he spoke to me and warned me that absolute obedience at all cost will be the price for having a share in the greatest wave of revival that ever has been known in history.[41]

What is most significant about this account is that it is truly before David was involved in this revival—or any of the traditional

41. David du Plessis, *By One Spirit into One Body*, 1, quoted in Robinson, "To the Ends of the Earth," 87.

churches were involved—as this did not happen until after his first meeting with Dr. MacKay and the World Council of Churches headquarters, which, as you will remember, took place in 1952.

Another likely reason that David had a hard time remembering the prophecy word for word was because of the nature of Brother Wigglesworth's delivery of what he had seen in his vision. David must have been somewhat in a state of shock while hearing it, as he was pinned to the wall by Smith's strong hands. Through the research of Father Peter Hocken, who has made the best attempt to date to document the original prophecy, it has been discovered that at least four different versions of this prophecy exist, all which differ slightly because of the time between the event and the writing and David's inadvertent addition of other things God had shown him through his meditations upon and walking out of the vision. According to Father Hocken's work, the four versions are found in David's autobiography, *A Man Called Mr. Pentecost* (1977), the souvenir brochure from the Third World Pentecostal Conference (1952), *As at the Beginning* (1965), and an article in *A Voice of Faith* (1964). The version in David's autobiography is the most official of these and is very similar to the one presented in his 1970 address (which appeared in the previous chapter), though it does have some additional details of what was spoken. From putting these four versions together using a somewhat unscientific and "educated guess" system, Father Hocken came up with the following approximation of what was said to David du Plessis as he stood pinned to the wall by Smith Wigglesworth:

> There is a revival coming that at present the world knows nothing about. It will come through the churches. It will come in a fresh way. When you see what God does in this

There is a revival coming that at present the world knows nothing about. It will come through the churches. It will come in a fresh way.

> revival, you will then have to admit that all you have seen previously is a mere nothing in comparison with what is to come. It will eclipse anything that has been known in history. Empty churches, empty cathedrals will be packed again with worshippers. Buildings will not be able to accommodate the multitudes. Then you will see fields of people worshipping and praising together. The Lord intends to use you in this revival. For you have been in Jerusalem long enough. The Lord will send you to the uttermost parts of the earth. If you are faithful and humble, the Lord will use you, and if you remain faithful and humble, you will see the greatest events in church history.[42]

While this lag in time might lead some to doubt the validity of this prophecy, there is some good evidence to corroborate it. The first is a conversation that was had with Smith Wigglesworth in New Zealand:

> In the book *New Zealand's Greatest Revival*...a brother remarked to Smith Wigglesworth: "One is tempted to envy you when you have had such great success."
>
> He received the following reply: "Young man, it is the other way around. I feel like envying you. I have had three visions in my life—three only. The first two have already come to pass, but the third is yet to be fulfilled. I will most likely pass on to my reward, but you are a young man and will most likely be in what I saw." He burst out, "Oh, it was amazing. Oh," he said, "I cannot tell God's secrets. But you remember what I say—this revival we have had is nothing to what God is yet going to do."

42. Peter Hocken, "Baptised in the Spirit: The Origins and Early Development of the Charismatic Movement in Great Britain" (Ph.D. Thesis, University of Birmingham, 1984), 2, in Martin, "To the Ends of the Earth," 87.

> The one to whom Brother Wigglesworth addressed these words commented: "It was quite evident that the evangelist had a special vision granted him of the coming outpouring of the Spirit in an unprecedented effusion in the days just before our Lord comes to snatch away the church."[43]

The second is the change that was brought to the life of David du Plessis. David would have been among the last to seek ecumenical ties because he grew up fighting them throughout his early ministry. It is somewhat similar to the change that was seen in Peter on the day of Pentecost. While Peter had been a coward and denied Christ three times on the night before Jesus' crucifixion, on the day of Pentecost he stepped up before the crowd and proclaimed that Jesus was the Messiah, to such effect that three thousand were saved that day. In the words of many who have looked at this situation, "Something definitely happened to inspire that change," and this is one of the evidences given time and again for the resurrection of Jesus. Something tremendous happened to make that change, and it couldn't have been the disciples stealing away Jesus' body in the dead of night, because Peter never could have come up with such conviction if he had known it was all a fraud. In the same way, we know something must have happened to David du Plessis to change his attitude toward the mainline denominations from being the enemies of Christ to being the main focus to whom Christ wanted him to reach out with love and forgiveness.

Because of these things, among others, researchers into the work of David du Plessis have not only come to the conclusion that the prophecy was genuine, but also that this prophecy was one of the most significant events of the twentieth century. It was the conception of the charismatic renewal that would bring the Pentecostal reawakening from fringe groups into the mainstream churches.

---

43. Gordon Lindsay, "Are the Gifts of the Spirit for the Church Today?" *Voice of Healing* (1963), 5, in Martin, "To the Ends of the Earth," 100.

While organizations, such as the Full Gospel Business Men's Fellowship, and ministries, such as Kathryn Kuhlman's, welcomed people of all denominations into their meetings and introduced them to the baptism in the Holy Spirit, David du Plessis was the one who gave doctrinal support—albeit not of a scholarly nature—to what they were doing (as to a somewhat lesser extent did Donald Gee and his writings) and was the voice to church leaders around the world that this was a move of the Spirit aligned with sound biblical interpretation. For this reason, the move was accepted rather than shut down in some of the most unexpected places, not the least of which was the Catholic Church. And, as a result, churches have filled to overflowing, and Pentecostalism has been one of the strongest missionary outreaches in the last several hundred years, including the mass revivals that began in Argentina in 1954 with Tommy Hicks and continue today in Africa in the ministry of Reinhard Bonnke.

More than this historical significance, though, is the fact that there is much to learn about prophecy—and fulfilling the prophecy of this word from Smith Wigglesworth, as well as the effect it had on the life of David du Plessis. For that reason, before going on to look at the vision given to Tommy Hicks and its implications for us today—the revival that is to come—it is worth taking the time to look further into the gift of prophecy and how we are to apply it in our own lives when we hear a prophetic word.

5

Fulfilling Prophecy

Blessed is he that readeth, and they that hear the words of this prophecy, and keep those things which are written therein: for the time is at hand....For the testimony of Jesus is the spirit of prophecy.
—Revelation 1:3; 19:10

The ultimate purpose of all prophecy is to lift up Jesus for the salvation of all who hear. The simple test of the soundness of prophecy is this: false prophecy will puff up the person or people hearing it, feeding their egos; true prophecy will lift up Christ. Thus, Smith Wigglesworth's conditions on his prophecy to David du Plessis ring true:

> God says all the things that I have told you already will come to pass, and you will see them, and you will have part in them, with only this condition, *that you remain humble and faithful.* If you can remember those two things—remain humble and faithful—then God will use you in a way that no one else is used, unusual, it will not be the trend, it will be you and God, and you must keep *humble* and remain *faithful.*[44]

The true purpose of this prophecy was not that David would have a huge international ministry—even though that is what it

44. The italics have been added to emphasize the point here.

turned out to be—but that he would have a new way to testify of Jesus Christ among traditional churches that had all but forgotten about His true nature and the ministry of His Holy Spirit.

The true purpose of this prophecy was not that David would have a huge international ministry—even though that is what it turned out to be—but that he would have a new way to testify of Jesus Christ among traditional churches.

Echoing this, in his teachings on prophecy (which are included as chapters 8 and 9 of this book[45]), Smith Wigglesworth establishes that there are three classes of prophecy and three purposes for it (subservient to the ultimate purpose of testifying of Jesus). In 1927, in a teaching presented to a group of Bible students at Angelus Temple in Los Angeles, Smith Wigglesworth identified the types of prophecy as being either 1) the testimony of a person who has been saved, 2) the words of a minister in a message spoken under the anointing of God, or 3) someone speaking out of the gift of prophecy through a vision or by the inspiration of the Holy Spirit. Considering these options, we see that Smith's prophecy to David falls into the third category. He also stated that, according to 1 Corinthians 14:3, prophecy is for the 1) edification, 2) exhortation, and 3) consolation of the hearers. When it is used for edification, it strengthens the believers as they humble themselves before Christ and enables them to do what God has called them to do. Exhortation directs and motivates them to act—there is something they need to do, whether that is responding to the message of salvation or acting upon something God has put in their hearts to do. Under prophecy that exhorts, it is also important to recognize that prophecy also instructs and informs. Sometimes prophecy instructs us in directions we should go, giving conditional directions in a sort of "If…, then…" format. A good deal of scriptural instruction falls into this category. One example is James 4:7–8:

45. It may be best to turn to these chapters and read them before continuing.

Submit yourselves therefore to God. Resist the devil, and he will flee from you. Draw nigh to God, and he will draw nigh to you.

Would you like the devil to flee from you? Then you must a) submit yourself to God and b) resist the devil. These two conditions are necessary before you can collect the promise of Satan fleeing from you. Do you want God to draw close to you? Then you must first draw close or seek after Him. As Jeremiah 29:13 says, "*Ye shall seek me, and find me, when ye shall search for me with all your heart.*" Other prophecy is unconditional and informs us of what is going to happen no matter how we act. The book of Revelation is this type of prophecy. In this light, Smith Wigglesworth's prophecy to David du Plessis was a bit of both. It was unconditional in that the revival he saw in the vision was coming no matter what people did. However, it was also conditional: if David wanted to be part of that revival, then he needed to stay humble and faithful. Thank God for all of us that he did. But, had he not, God would have found someone else to fill that role in the charismatic renewal.

Lastly, prophecy is for consolation—helping believers recover from setbacks or loss by reemphasizing God's love for them and His power to redeem them from whatever they may be facing and to bring comfort to the situation. Again, in this context, Smith Wigglesworth's prophecy to David du Plessis includes at least two of these three: edification to know that God had called him to a specific task and exhortation to act on it and stay humble and faithful so that he could accomplish it. There may also have been a note of consolation in that David would also be healed of the pains inflicted previously by the mainline denominations—specifically the Dutch Reformed ministers—and that he would be reconciled with these congregations that had initially opposed the Pentecostal movement. Of course, this was much easier to see in retrospect than in 1936, or even in 1950, when David was just embarking on what would become his part in the charismatic renewal of the 1950s, 1960s, and

1970s. It is one thing to look back and see how prophecy worked, but it is quite another to hear it and know how to act upon it. How are we to judge prophecy so that we may discern how to act upon it?

Judging Prophecy

The first rule of judging prophecy is still the best: Does the word puff up the hearer or lift up Christ? As John said in his first epistle:

> *Beloved, believe not every spirit, but try the spirits whether they are of God: because many false prophets are gone out into the world. Hereby know ye the Spirit of God: Every spirit that confesseth that Jesus Christ is come in the flesh is of God: And every spirit that confesseth not that Jesus Christ is come in the flesh is not of God: and this is that spirit of antichrist, whereof ye have heard that it should come; and even now already is it in the world.* (1 John 4:1–3)

Any spirit that denies either Jesus' full physical incarnation in coming to earth or His full deity as part of the Godhead is not from God. Any spirit that speaks of the greatness of the hearer to touch his ego rather than touch his spirit is not lifting up Christ and is not from God. Such are spirits that seek to deceive rather than edify, exhort, or console with the goal of bringing hearers to kneel at the foot of the cross.

Any spirit that denies either Jesus' full physical incarnation in coming to earth or His full deity as part of the Godhead is not from God.

A second test is whether or not the word of prophecy aligns with specific Scriptures or principles of the Bible. What was David's first question to Smith Wigglesworth when he came back after delivering this prophecy? "Brother Wigglesworth, I am really amazed, and I just want to ask you, *have you got Scripture for such a thing?"*[46] When he posed this question, Smith Wigglesworth gave him the scriptural examples of what he had seen in his vision.

Just as with following Jesus, the Pentecostal movement would first be a fisherman's—or layperson's—movement among those hungriest for all that God had to give, and then it would be a priestly movement among those who had long professed God but rejected Him when they met Him face-to-face. Just as the Pharisees and Sadducees rejected Jesus because they clung to their false interpretations of the Scriptures rather than seeing the truth in His, the mainline denominations missed the Holy Spirit when He came for a renewal of Pentecost through Azusa Street and similar places. And, just as many of the priests came to Christ after His resurrection, many in the mainline denominations would accept the baptism of the Holy Spirit once they saw the fruit it had produced in the lives of other believers. No spoken prophecy that is from God will contradict the teachings of the Bible. To emphasize this further, we need to look at what Peter said in his second epistle to the churches:

> *For we have not followed cunningly devised fables, when we made known unto you the power and coming of our Lord Jesus Christ, but were eyewitnesses of his majesty. For he received from God the Father honour and glory, when there came such a voice to him from the excellent glory, This is my beloved Son, in whom I am well pleased. And this voice which came from heaven we heard, when we were with him in the holy mount.* ***We have also a more sure word of prophecy****; whereunto ye do well that ye take heed, as unto a light that shineth in a dark place, until the day dawn, and the day star arise in your hearts:* ***Knowing this first, that no prophecy of the scripture is of any private interpretation. For the prophecy came not in old time by the will of man: but holy men of God spake as they were moved by the Holy Ghost.***

46. The italics have been added for emphasis.

> *But there were false prophets also among the people, even as there shall be false teachers among you, who privily shall bring in damnable heresies, even denying the Lord that bought them, and bring upon themselves swift destruction. And many shall follow their pernicious ways; by reason of whom the way of truth shall be evil spoken of. And* ***through covetousness shall they with feigned words make merchandise of you:*** *whose judgment now of a long time lingereth not, and their damnation slumbereth not.*
>
> (2 Peter 1:16–2:3, emphasis added)

Peter pointed out a couple of very interesting facts about prophecy in this passage. The first is that no prophecy is of private interpretation, meaning that all prophecy will agree with all other prophecy, and New Testament prophecy will be understood by the believer through his or her relationship with Christ. New Testament prophecy differs from what was given in the Old Testament because, under the new covenant, prophecy is spoken to believers who have the Holy Spirit dwelling inside of them; under the old covenant, prophets spoke by the unction of the Holy Spirit to people who did not have the Spirit of God dwelling within them. Old Testament believers had the law dictated to them, not written on their hearts; New Testament believers have God's law inscribed in their hearts and have been given the Holy Spirit within them to confirm it and guide them.

Any prophecy given to an individual under the new covenant must bear witness with the Spirit dwelling in him.

Any prophecy given to an individual under the new covenant must *bear witness* with the Spirit dwelling in him. What has been said will be confirmed by the Spirit in his heart. Prophecy will be realized not by the person seeking to make it happen but simply through the believer continuing to follow God with all his heart, mind, soul, and strength. We should never pursue prophecy; we must always pursue Christ.

Many mistakes were made regarding prophecy in what has come to be known as the shepherding movement, where believers were encouraged to follow the "prophecies" and counsel of their leaders as if they were still under the old covenant.[47] These "prophecies" spoke of whom one should marry, business deals one should make, ministries one should embark upon, and other similar details, often with quite disastrous results. The mistake was that people pursued the "prophecies" instead of God. When a prophecy turned out to be false, regardless of the sincerity of the person who delivered it, the hearer was led away from Christ instead of toward Him.

An example occurred in the life of David du Plessis when he first met Anna and the Lord told him she would one day be his wife. Although this was a specific word from the Lord, David did not act upon it by asking her to marry him the next day. Rather, he let things run their normal course and courted her for eighteen months before they married. He allowed the word of the Lord to be confirmed in him by following the wisdom of Scripture and not rushing things but instead practicing patience and preferring Anna above himself. As a result, their marriage lasted nearly sixty years.

Biblical Examples of Specific Prophecy

To cultivate an even deeper understanding of this, it is worth looking at three New Testament examples of prophecy given to individuals or groups. The first is Agabus' prophecy to Paul in Acts:

> *And as we tarried there* [in Caesarea] *many days, there came down from Judaea a certain prophet, named Agabus. And when he was come unto us, he took Paul's girdle, and bound his own hands and feet, and said, Thus saith the Holy Ghost,*

47. It is worth noting here that David du Plessis was asked to take part in the initial 1975 meetings that helped right this "discipleship movement" and get its followers back onto a more correct course.

So shall the Jews at Jerusalem bind the man that owneth this girdle, and shall deliver him into the hands of the Gentiles. (Acts 21:10–11)

God sent Agabus to confirm what was already in Paul's heart: that he was to go to Jerusalem to be arrested, imprisoned, and eventually taken to Rome to bear witness of Jesus. It is interesting to note that those who heard the message with Paul interpreted it as a warning that Paul was not to go to Jerusalem, while Paul alone knew that it was the course God was planning for him and that Agabus' words were not only confirmation of what lay ahead of him but also assurance that it was God's will and that He would be with Paul through it all. We see this later confirmed after Paul is imprisoned in Jerusalem and the Lord comes to speak to him:

And the night following the Lord stood by him, and said, Be of good cheer, Paul: for as thou hast testified of me in Jerusalem, so must thou bear witness also at Rome. (Acts 23:11)

A second example of specific prophecy is the words Christ spoke through John to the seven churches of Asia in the first few chapters of the book of Revelation. When you read these, you very much see these prophecies edifying, exhorting, or consoling. In each, the Lord speaks of the church's strengths and then gives correction and exhortation to return to first principles or "correct course" back to what He has called it to do. We also see consolation in each, ending with Christ virtually throwing His arms open to welcome them back in, or, as He so aptly put it to the Laodiceans:

As many as I love, I rebuke and chasten: be zealous therefore, and repent. Behold, I stand at the door, and knock: if any man hear my voice, and open the door, I will come in to him, and will sup with him, and he with me. To him that overcometh will I grant to sit with me in my throne, even as I also overcame,

and am set down with my Father in his throne. He that hath an ear, let him hear what the Spirit saith unto the churches.
(Revelation 3:19–22)

The third prophecy I would like to offer as an example is not actually included in the Scriptures, but it is referred to in Paul's letters to Timothy:

This charge I commit unto thee, son Timothy, according to the prophecies which went before on thee, that thou by them mightest war a good warfare; holding faith, and a good conscience; which some having put away concerning faith have made shipwreck....Neglect not the gift that is in thee, which was given thee by prophecy, with the laying on of the hands of the presbytery. Meditate upon these things; give thyself wholly to them; that thy profiting may appear to all. Take heed unto thyself, and unto the doctrine; continue in them: for in doing this thou shalt both save thyself, and them that hear thee.
(1 Timothy 1:18–19; 4:14–16)

And Paul echoed again in his second letter to him:

Wherefore I put thee in remembrance that thou stir up the gift of God, which is in thee by the putting on of my hands. For God hath not given us the spirit of fear; but of power, and of love, and of a sound mind. Be not thou therefore ashamed of the testimony of our Lord, nor of me his prisoner: but be thou partaker of the afflictions of the gospel according to the power of God; who hath saved us, and called us with an holy calling, not according to our works, but according to his own purpose and grace. (2 Timothy 1:6–9)

In these passages, we see that Paul's advice to Timothy is to "*meditate upon these things, give thyself wholly to them....Take heed to thyself, and unto doctrine, continue in them.*" Thus, he asked him to meditate upon the prophecies spoken over him, aligning them with doctrine (for Timothy had no New Testament to refer to at this time), giving himself to these good things, while also "taking heed to himself," or measuring them by the Holy Spirit inside of him. If he did these things, then, according to Paul, he would save both himself and those who heard him. In the second letter, Paul also told him to stir up these gifts, finding courage from the spirit of power, love, and common sense within himself. Why? Because he had been called with a holy calling and enabled by God to bring it to pass. Was he to force these things to happen? No, he was to mediate on them, ponder them, and be ready to follow God into them as they were confirmed in his own heart through the Holy Spirit within him.

It is perhaps this last example that best parallels what David du Plessis experienced in Smith Wiggleworth's prophecy to him. First of all, it was given far in advance of its fulfillment so that David had plenty of time to think about it and ponder what it meant. Over the course of his meditation, God began to change attitudes in David's heart that needed to be changed before he became the man who could fulfill God's calling on his life. David also waited on God to open the doors and lead him before he began walking out the vision of what Smith had told him he would be doing with the majority of his life as a minister. He found himself taking gradual steps toward being the reconciler God had called him to be, first among the Pentecostals and then among all of the churches, even those so liberal they had become apostate. This leads to another major point about prophecy that David learned as God spoke to him and as he prayed and recovered in the hospital after his car accident: that prophecy is meaningless if it is not applied with love and forgiveness.

Over the course of his meditation, God began to change attitudes in David's heart that needed to be changed before he became the man who could fulfill God's calling on his life.

Prophecy Is Nothing Without Love

In the heart of his letter to the Corinthians in which he taught about spiritual gifts, Paul interjects the greatest discourse on the love of God found in the Bible. Of these Scriptures in 1 Corinthians 13, we tend to focus on verses 4–8, but look for a moment at what is written on either side of that famous passage:

> *And though I have the gift of prophecy, and understand all mysteries, and all knowledge; and though I have all faith, so that I could remove mountains, and have not charity* [love], *I am nothing....Charity* [love] *never faileth: but* ***whether there be prophecies, they shall fail;*** *whether there be tongues, they shall cease; whether there be knowledge, it shall vanish away. For we know in part, and we prophesy in part. But when that which is perfect is come, then that which is in part shall be done away.* (1 Corinthians 13:2, 8–10, emphasis added)

Too often we are so fascinated by what is revealed in prophecy—in the power and wonder of truth uncovered—that we forget that if the truth is not applied in love, it is nothing. David's earliest instincts in hearing this Scripture were that he would march into ecumenical circles with the truth of God's Word and correct them as Jonah corrected the people of Nineveh. He was right, and they were wrong. He would go in and preach the truth, and they would fall to their knees, repenting in sackcloth and ashes, or be destroyed by the hand of the Lord. But, because of the cross, God no longer operates that way. The truth was to be offered in love, and in order to bring repentance, David first had to learn to offer forgiveness by forgiving those from the traditional denominations who had hurt him as a young Pentecostal.

Without love, prophecy will fail and come to an end, because we don't know it all—we see only in part and must walk out the rest by following the "God of love who is love."[48] Again, prophecy that creates pride is either false or misused; it is only prophecy that brings people closer to Christ and His love that is true.

In the Final Analysis

By considering these things, there is a great deal to be learned from the prophecy God gave through Smith Wigglesworth to David du Plessis and what God was hoping to see come of the Pentecostal/charismatic movements. God was not looking to create a new denomination but to reunify all believers in the bond of the Spirit. In many senses, it is easy to call this a failure, because, in the end, denominations divided further, creating a greater number; however, in a more important sense, it was a tremendous success. Through what has been sifted and separated into different movements—notably, what has been called the Pentecostal movement, the ecumenical movement, neo-Pentecostalism, and the charismatic renewal, the work has been done all by the same Spirit, and there is now a body of that Spirit within literally all the Christian denominations and paradenominations of the earth, which, according to the *World Christian Encyclopedia*, number nearly 34,000.[49] The key to true unity is not becoming more like each other but each of us becoming more like Jesus, which is the primary work that the Holy Spirit does in anyone's life.

The key to true unity is not becoming more like each other but each of us becoming more like Jesus, which is the primary work that the Holy Spirit does in anyone's life.

While "The Smith Wigglesworth Prophecy," as it has come to be known over time, has raised incredible interest because of the man who gave it and the revival it foretold, it is important to

48. See 1 John 4:8; 16.
49. Barrett et al., ed., *World Christian Encyclopedia*, 10.

remember that it was not a prophecy for all of us. It was a prophetic word given specifically to David du Plessis so that he could ponder it, be changed by it, and, in the end, give himself wholly to it when it looked as if all of the rest of his brethren had forsaken him because of it. It is also important that the rest of us allow such men as David du Plessis to follow God when they are called to do so. It is an unfortunate mistake that his ordination papers were pulled by the Assemblies of God just as his ministry was peaking. And it is also unfortunate that Rev. du Plessis is not the only minister to whom this happened when he broke away from the mainstream to follow the voice of God.

Ordination is the recognition of God's call upon a life, not a means of trying to control someone and prevent any actions we may not fully support. It is good that the Assemblies of God later reinstated him, as has also happened with many others in similar circumstances, but it is nevertheless unfortunate that they were cast aside in the first place.

For a time, especially in the late 1950s and early 1960s, when David's ordination papers had been revoked, it was only David, God, and what God had spoken to him through Smith Wigglesworth. Of course, out of this, the important thing was that it was David and God, not David and the prophecy, for had he not continued to pursue God through it all—had he pursued the prophecy instead—it very well could have been the others who were right in pulling his papers, and not David.

However, the fact remains that this prophecy was specifically for David du Plessis—and it was fulfilled. Other prophecies, however—such as the one given to Tommy Hicks, which we will discuss in the next section—were given more generally to the church and are still waiting for us to rise up and take part in their fulfillment. It is for this reason that we include the Tommy Hicks prophecy—it is one of the best capsulations existing, in our estimation, of prophecies about the final worldwide revival that will take place before Jesus returns to the earth. By taking what we have discussed in this first section and applying it to ourselves and to the prophecy given through Tommy Hicks, it is clear that we still have a lot to do as we approach what will truly be the greatest revival of all time.

Tommy Hicks

Part II

The Vision of the "Awakening Giant" Given to Tommy Hicks

6

Tommy Hicks and the Great Argentine Revival

It is not necessary for us to examine the life of Tommy Hicks as closely as we did that of David du Plessis in order to understand the vision God gave to him. However, it is important to understand why God gave this message to Tommy Hicks and not anyone else. It is equally important to understand that the magnitude of what Tommy experienced in 1954 in Buenos Aires—which appeared to be the greatest single set of revival meetings in the history of the world to date (and was later surpassed in the 1990s by Reinhard Bonnke's meetings in Africa, where he saw millions saved)—made him the perfect man to speak this vision through. What he had witnessed in South America gave him only the smallest glimmer of what God intends to do on the earth before Jesus returns.

Another important factor is the state of Argentina in 1954. Unaffected by the destruction of World War II, Argentina was among the ten most prosperous nations of the world at the time, even exceeding some European countries. President Juan Domingo Perón, who was a central figure in Argentine politics from 1944 until his death in 1974, was at the peak of his career—the following year, he would be ousted in a military coup and exiled—and Argentina was confident about its future. This was no backward, third-world country; Argentina was alive and prospering, and was as arrogant as any Western nation claiming similar success. Not only that, but up until the meetings organized by Tommy Hicks, the nation had proven one of the most resistant to the gospel. Yet, for two months, beginning the week before Easter 1954 and running through June 13, God showed the Argentines that they still had great needs only He could meet.

Believers in Argentina had begun praying and believing for these meetings in 1951. In the succeeding years, roughly thirty churches in Buenos Aires pulled together to back and promote the event, which would begin April 14, 1954. At the same time, God had put the nation of Argentina on the heart of Rev. Tommy Hicks, who arrived at the Los Angeles airport for a flight bound for Buenos Aires with his airline ticket, luggage, and $47. However, before he even got on the plane, he was blessed by others who had gathered to send him off, and he left the United States full of purpose.

The coalition of churches had hoped to have Rev. T. L. Osborn speak at the gathering, but he was unavailable, and so they asked Tommy to speak. Pastor Paul Sorensen, a native of Argentina, was asked to interpret. In preparation, they printed 80,000 flyers, 1,000 large posters, and 20,000 church guides; placed a large ad in a local paper with distribution to 300,000 people; traveled among the churches to promote the event; and rented the stadium of the Atlanta Football (Soccer) Club, which seated 45,000. When close to 8,000 people showed up for the first night's meeting, they were quite pleased. It was the largest evangelical gathering in the history of the nation. Tommy spoke with authority and anointing, and there were some wonderful healings. Everyone was pleased with the outcome. But God was just getting started.

The next night, there were close to 9,000 attendees at the meeting, and many were surprised. Even those who had initially opposed the meetings started to take notice. Rev. Hicks preached on the healing of the Syrophenician woman's daughter,[50] and "we

50. See Mark 7:25–30.

could almost see that happy little lady running down the dusty road to meet her delivered daughter."[51] Again, there were remarkable healings.

The number of attendees remained steady through Friday, when they started allowing those who had been healed to step up to the microphone and testify. The following night, attendance was at least 10,000, and at the Easter Sunday afternoon meeting, it exceeded 12,000. Photographers from the local papers were present, worship was growing stronger, and many deaf and dumb were healed, among other ailments. On Monday of that week, the numbers did not dwindle at all—again, more than 12,000 were in attendance. Rev. Hicks spoke on faith and healing, and hundreds openly accepted Jesus as Lord and Savior. There were more healings, including those of several paralytics who praised God loudly before the crowd. Another man was delivered from a demon and was so changed that when he returned the next night, even Rev. Hicks and his family couldn't recognize him. That night, T. L. and Daisy Osborn were able to join them, and Rev. Osborn spoke for about twenty minutes. Healings and testimonies continued to flow. The numbers were growing so much that other ministers were asked to join in helping to pray for people. One young Argentine pastor was surprised when a paralytic began to walk after he had prayed for him.

More ads and flyers were printed and distributed, and the meetings continued to grow. This was now by far the greatest spiritual movement Argentina had ever seen. So many healings were taking place that it was impossible to record them all. A new chorus was sung in Spanish and adopted as the theme chorus for the meetings: "Argentina, a redeemed country,/ That's the theme of our faithful churches./ Let's raise up the banner of Christ!/ Then transformed Argentines will be seen."[52]

---

51. Stokes, *The Great Revival in Buenos Aires*, 7.
52. Ibid., 12.

Police escort Tommy Hicks through a crowd at Atlanta Stadium.

One of the crowds at Atlanta Stadium in Buenos Aires

Tommy at a meeting of the Full Gospel Business Men's Fellowship with its founder, Demos Shakarian, on the right

BUENOS AIRES HERALD — Tuesday, May 25, 1

FAITH HEALER PACKS T HURACAN STADIUM

Day-long Wait To Pray With Evangelist Hicks

(BY A HERALD REPORTER)

TWO hundred thousand persons, men, women and children, many with babes in arms, filled the Huracan Football Club Stadium last evening, to listen to Thomas Hicks, Evangelist Faith-Healer.

From the early hours of the morning hundreds waited for the stadium gates to open. In the evening approaching 19 o'clock, automobiles, taxis, buses and colectivos turned off Caseros into calle Colonia and thence towards Figueroa Alcorta.

ROADS JAMMED

At Plaza Constitución half an hour after the meeting had commenced, it was practically impossible to travel either by tram or bus in the direction of the stadium. All seemed to be making that way.

The scene in Colonia and the Avenida Figueroa Alcorta was an impressive one. Cadillacs and latest model Plymouths lined the streets together with ancient Fords, lorries and large buses. Stationary

ed around the entrance, swarming up the steps and blocking all gangways.

The Intendente of the Huracan Club, however, solved all difficulties, and following him down below through the players' dressing-rooms and then up the steps to the playing pitch, an impressive sight met the eye.

SOLITARY FIGURE

Under the stars and the glittering overhead arc lamps of the club a solitary figure stood alone in a large expanse of green grass and looked around at the thousands of faces all of these looking in his direction.

Among the huge gathering, one saw the crippled and the blind, the sick and

ing on stretchers there in hired am and old people in chairs. But not all or ill.

"Alleluia" said English. Immedia peated in Spanish luia" responded dred thousand voice your arms to God," and four hundred arms were raised sky.

"Stand still and heads in prayer." lence was impressiv

"Jesus Christ is th lation of God in the said the preacher, words echoed and round the stadium words were repeate

— Blind men cove sightless eyes w hand as the other ed upwards, the and the crippled rise and use the mothers held th and deformed high-up in their mute appeal to G

And then the wh dium burst out int sounding clapping followed by all si hymn

While thousands others slowly mad way down the gang wards the street.

Newspaper article describing the revival

Tommy Hicks, shown with his interpreter, Paul Sorenson, and those they addressed at Atlanta Stadium.

A sea of faces at the Great Huracán Stadium

Tommy shakes hands with John Osteen after a speaking engagement.

Argentines raising their hands to receive Christ as Savior

Rev. Hicks meets an admiring crowd.

Tommy with a crusade team; Demos Shakarian is at the far right.

Tommy Hicks with a group of Argentine ministers in 1954
On the far right is Louie W. Stokes, who recorded the results of Tommy's ministry in his book *The Great Revival in Buenos Aires.*

On Saturday afternoon, April 24, attendance had grown to about 13,000, and Rev. Hicks spoke on John 11, "I am the Resurrection and the Life." At least 3,000 had publicly professed Christ so far in the campaign. The stadium was closing in on being about one-third full. Other churches began joining the coalition that sponsored the event, and Rev. Hicks was even asked to speak at a Bible school in town. Despite the cold and rainy weather, the crowds stayed faithful, although they dwindled back to about 10,000 again. God was not through, however.

Left to right: Hal Herman, Howard Carter, Tommy Hicks, and Ben Kummerfeld in June 1955

On May 1, which was Labor Day in Argentina, no public meetings were allowed, so Rev. Hicks spoke to a gathering of pastors in the Assembly of God Hall about organizing a Full Gospel Business Men's group in Buenos Aires. The message was well received.

Then, on Sunday, May 2, the rain ceased, and the floodgates began to open. Over 20,000 people came to the meeting, and God continued to save and heal. Tommy preached a message entitled "God Has Always Delivered His People." Over a thousand people signed cards saying they had been born again. These cards began to be distributed to the local churches so that the leaders could follow up with them and get them connected to faithful churches in the area. Again, there were more sick people present than could be prayed for at the platform, so prayer was offered for them wherever they sat, and many more healings took place. By Wednesday of that week, the crowd numbered more than 30,000. Now, news of the meetings was spreading all over the country simply by word of mouth. By May 7, the audience was nearing 40,000. Churches were gathering together to offer prayer and counseling.

By Sunday, it was evident that they were outgrowing the capacity of the stadium. By Tuesday of that week, May 11, attendance was between 60,000 and 70,000, with people standing in the aisles and out in the streets surrounding the stadium. The next night, an estimated 80,000 to 100,000 flocked to the meeting. Newspapers ran lengthy articles about the event, and a *Time-Life* reporter was even present. But God still was not through. Soon, there were more people outside the stadium, listening in, than present inside. For ten consecutive nights, attendance was estimated to exceed 100,000. Publishing houses were being cleared of their stocks of Bibles and Christian literature, such that these materials had to be flown in to meet the urgent demand for them.

On Saturday, May 22, the meetings were moved to the stadium of the Huracán soccer team, which could seat 110,000. This place filled, as well, and thousands still stood outside. On May 24, the local papers reported that attendance had surpassed 200,000. Such incredible crowds continued until the meetings closed on June 13. Local churches were filled beyond capacity, and the Buenos Aires Assembly of God had been forced to schedule five services on Sundays just to accommodate the increase in attendance. They were forced to rent a larger hall nearer the center of town to hold services. New churches were being opened everywhere, and the demand for Bibles and Christian literature had never been higher. Among those healed was the nephew of the vice president, who was healed of asthma, and a local publisher, Jose Luis Navarro, who was healed of rheumatism.

In the end, conservative estimates suggested that roughly three million people attended the meetings, some 50,000 Bibles and New Testaments had been printed and distributed, and about 300,000 salvation cards had been signed and distributed to the local churches. Innumerable people had heard the word of salvation for the first time, and countless people had been healed or delivered. The world had never seen such a revival before.

Innumerable people had heard the word of salvation for the first time, and countless people had been healed or delivered. The world had never seen such a revival before.

In the following years, the Full Gospel Business Men's Fellowship supported Tommy's return to Argentina in 1955, as well as funded several other revival meetings he led around the world, in Switzerland, Germany, New Zealand, Finland, and Russia. However, while miracles, healings, and salvations continued to manifest in his meetings as he preached, the results he saw never came close to matching what had happened in 1954 in Argentina. Between 1956 and 1958, Tommy also published three books that were largely made up of testimonies from his meetings and his teachings. Tommy passed away in 1973.

Tommy, perhaps more than anyone else, must have realized that something special had happened in Argentina the first time he went there, and that it had been a glimpse into what God had planned for later—a larger glimpse of which he would see in the vision given to him in 1961, which is recorded in the next chapter. It was an answer to the prayers of the churches of Argentina, but it was also something much more than that—a glimpse of God acting sovereignly to unleash heaven on earth. The Buenos Aires revival of which Tommy Hicks was privileged to be a major part was, in many ways, the beginning of God's last great revival on the earth.

7

The "Awakening Giant" Vision Given to Tommy Hicks

(Note: Rev. Tommy Hicks ministered this vision at a Full Gospel Business Men's Meeting in Los Angeles, California. It was later transcribed and printed into a booklet, entitled Vision Given to Tommy Hicks, Evangelist, July 25, 1961. The material in this chapter is adapted from that booklet.)

The message that I bring to you this morning is perhaps the most important thing—or one of the most important things—that ever happened to me in my life. I have had many tremendous experiences with God—God has been good to me. He has led me in paths that few of us have ever had the privilege of walking in.

My message begins July 25, 1961, about two thirty in the morning. I was in Winnipeg, Canada. I had hardly fallen asleep when the vision and the revelation that God gave to me came before me. The vision came three times, exact in detail, the morning of July 25, 1961. I was so stirred and so moved by the revelation that I tell you this morning, it has changed my complete outlook upon the body of Christ and upon the end-time ministry. I feel this morning that the greatest thing of the church lies straight ahead. It is so hard this morning to help men and women to realize and understand the thing that God is trying to give *His* people in the end time.

I received a letter several weeks ago from one of our native evangelists down in Africa—in Nairobi. This man and his wife were on their way up to Tanganyika. They could neither read, nor could they write, but we have been supporting them for over two years. And as they entered into the territory of Tanganyika, they came across a small village. The entire village was evacuating and leaving because of a plague that had hit that village. This man came across natives who were weeping and crying, and he asked them what was wrong. They told him their mother and father had suddenly died. They had been dead for three days, and they had to leave. They were afraid to go inside—they were leaving them in the cottage. He turned and asked them where they were. They pointed to the hut, and he asked them to go with him, but they refused. They were afraid to go. This native and his wife went to this little cottage—they entered into this cottage where the man and woman had been dead for three days. The evangelist simply stretched forth his hand in the name of the Lord Jesus Christ and spoke that man's name and that woman's name, and said, "In the name of the Lord Jesus Christ, I command life to come back to your bodies." Instantaneously, these two heathen people who had never known Jesus Christ as their Savior sat up and immediately began to praise God. The Spirit and the power of God came into the life of these people. To us, that may seem strange and may seem a phenomenon. But that is a beginning of this end-time ministry.

God is going to take the "do-nothings," the "nobodies," the "unheard-ofs," the "no-accounts"—He is going to take every man and every woman—and He is going to give to them this outpouring of the Spirit of God. In the book of Acts, we read, *"In the last days, saith God, I will pour out of my Spirit upon all flesh."*[53] Do you believe that this morning?

I wonder this morning if we realize what God meant when He said, *"I will pour out of my Spirit upon all flesh."* I do not think I fully

53. Acts 2:17.

realize, nor could I understand, the fullness of it. And then I read from the book of Joel: "*Be glad then, ye children of Zion, and rejoice in the* Lord *your God: for he hath given you the former rain moderately, and he will cause to come down for you the rain, the former rain, and the latter rain....*"[54] It is not only going to be the rain, the former and the latter rain, but He is going to give to His people—and I believe with all my heart—in these last days, we are going to receive a double portion of the power of God. And, I say again, it is hard for us to realize, because we living, as it were, in that lethargy and in that sleepiness.

People do not always understand what you say, but they can feel what you have.

We do not realize what God is trying to do. And yet, all over the world, men and women—like the native workers who went into Tanganyika—they could not even read or write and had to have someone else to read their Bible for them, but they knew the Lord Jesus Christ. People do not always understand what you say, but they can feel what you have. Peter turned to the lame man at the Gate Beautiful, and he said, "That which I have, I give unto thee. In the name of the Lord Jesus Christ, stand up and walk."[55] We are going to see such demonstrations as the world has never seen. I believe it, and I know it with all of my heart.

As the vision appeared to me, after I was asleep, I suddenly found myself in a great high distance. Where I was, I do not know. But, as I was looking down upon the earth, suddenly, the whole world came into view—every nation, every kindred, and every tongue came before my sight, from the east and from the west, from the north and the south; and I recognized every country, and many cities that I had been in...and I was almost in fear and trembling as I stood beholding the great sight before me. And at that moment, when the world came into view, it began to lightning and thunder.

54. Joel 2:23.
55. See Acts 3:6.

And as the lightning flashed over the face of the earth, my eyes went downward—I was facing the north. And suddenly I beheld what looked like a great giant, and I stared and looked at it. I was almost bewildered by the sight. It was so gigantic and so great in stature; its feet seemed to reach to the North Pole, and its head to the south; its arms were stretched from sea to sea. I could not even begin to understand whether this was a mountain or whether this was a giant. But, as I watched it, I suddenly beheld this great giant; I could see it was struggling for life, to even live. But its body was covered with debris from head to foot; and, at times, this great giant would move its body and act as though it would rise up.

And when it did, thousands of little creatures seemed to run away—hideous-looking creatures would run away from this giant—and when it would become calm, they would come back.

All of a sudden, this giant lifted its hand towards the heavens, and then it lifted its other hand. And when it did, these creatures by the thousands seemed to flee away from this giant and go out into the darkness and into the night. Slowly this great giant began to rise, and as it did, its head and hands went into the clouds. As it rose to its feet, it seemed to have cleansed itself from the debris and filth that were upon it, and it began to raise its hands into the heavens, as though praising the Lord. And as it raised its hands, it was even unto the clouds.

Suddenly, every cloud became silver—the most beautiful silver that I have ever known. As I watched the phenomenon—it was so great—I could not even begin to understand what it all meant. I was so stirred as I watched it. And I cried to the Lord, and I said, "Oh Lord, what is the meaning of this?" And it felt as if I was actually in the Spirit, and I could feel the presence of the Lord—even as I was asleep.

And from those clouds, suddenly, great drops of liquid light began to rain down upon this mighty giant. And slowly, this giant began to melt—began to sink, as it were, into the very earth itself. And as it melted, its whole form seemed to have melted upon the face of the earth. And this great rain began to come down; liquid drops of light, as it were, began to flood the very earth itself. And as I watched, this giant that seemed to melt—suddenly it became millions of people over the face of the earth. As I beheld the sight before me, people stood up all over the world; they were lifting their hands, and they were praising the Lord.

At that very moment, there came a great thunder that seemed to roar from the heavens: a voice like that of a lion that roared. I turned my eyes toward the heavens, and suddenly I saw a figure in white, in glistening white—the most glorious thing that I have ever seen in all my life. I did not see the face, but somehow I knew that it was the Lord Jesus Christ. Somehow I knew it was Jesus Himself. And He stretched forth His hand. As He did so, He would stretch it forth to one, and to another, and to another; He stretched forth His hand upon the peoples and the nations of the world, men and women. As He pointed towards them, this liquid light seemed to flow from His hand into this person, and a mighty anointing of God came upon him or her. And those people began to go forth in the name of the Lord.

I do not know how long I watched it. It seemed it went into days and weeks and months. And I beheld this Christ; He continued to stretch forth His hand. But there was a tragedy. There were many people, as He stretched forth His hand, who refused the anointing of God and the call of God. I saw many women I knew, people whom I felt certainly would receive the call of God, but, as He stretched forth His hand toward this one, and toward that one, they simply bowed their heads and began to back away. And to each of those who seemed to bow down and back away, he or she seemed to go into darkness. Blackness seemed to swallow them everywhere.

I was bewildered as I watched it. But these people He had anointed—hundreds and thousands of people all over the world, in Africa, Asia, Russia, China, America, all over the world—the anointing of God was upon these peoples as they went forth in the name of the Lord. I saw these men and women as they went forth—they were ditch diggers, they were washermen, they were rich men, they were poor men; I saw people who were bound with paralysis, and sickness, and blindness; as the Lord stretched forth His hand to give them this anointing, they became well, they became healed, and they went forth.

And this is the miracle of it—this is the glorious miracle of it: those people would stretch forth their hand exactly as the Lord did. And it seemed that there was this liquid fire that seemed to be in their hand. As they stretched forth their hand, they said, "According to my word, be thou made whole."

I had hardly uttered those words when, somehow, something within me seemed to say; "The hour is coming, the day is coming, and you will see it—when you will stretch forth your hand—when My people will stretch forth their hands and these people shall be made whole."

I saw people go into insane institutions. This is all in the revelation that God gave me—it was so mighty and so majestic. I saw a little woman in a little gingham dress go stand in an insane institution. And as I saw her go into an insane institution, my mind went back to more than thirty years ago, in a little town in Illinois, when I had gone into an institution of some 500 inmates. In this insane institution, I remembered going from ward to ward, and as I looked at those people, tears streamed down my face, and I asked, "Oh Lord, why is it that Your people do not have power? Why is it that I do not have power that I could go in this institution and say: 'Be thou made whole'?" But I had hardly uttered those words when, somehow, something within me seemed to say; "The hour is coming, the day is coming, and you will see it—when you will stretch forth your hand—when My people will stretch forth their hands and these people shall be made whole."

As these people continued in this mighty end-time ministry, I did not fully realize what it was. And I looked to the Lord and said, "What is the meaning of this?" And He said, "This is that which I will do in the last days. I will restore all that the cankerworm, the palmerworm, the caterpillar—I will restore all that they have destroyed. This is My people. In the end time, they shall go forth. As a mighty army shall they sweep over the face of the earth."[56]

As I was at this great height—where I was, I do not know; whether I was a witness suspended in the air, I know not—I only know that I could behold the whole world. I watched these people as they were going to and fro over the face of the earth. Suddenly, here was a man in Africa, and in a moment he was transported in the Spirit of God, and perhaps he was in Russia, or in China, or in America, or in some other place, and vice versa—all over the world—these people went. And they came through fire, and through pestilence, and through famine. Neither fire nor persecution—nothing seemed to stop them.

Angry mobs came to them with swords and with guns, and, like Jesus, they passed through the multitude, and they could not find them. But they went forth in the name of the Lord....And everywhere they stretched forth their hands, the sick were healed, the blind eyes were opened. There was not a long prayer. And one of the things that occurred to me—after I had reviewed the vision so many times in my mind and thought about it so many times—I never saw a church, and I never saw or heard of a denomination; but these people were going in the name of the Lord of Hosts. Hallelujah!

As they marched forward, everything they did as the ministry of Christ in the end time. These people were ministering to the multitudes over the face of the earth. Tens of thousands, even millions,

56. See Joel 2.

seemed to come to the Lord Jesus Christ. These people stood forth and gave the message of the kingdom—of the coming kingdom—in this last hour. It was so glorious.

It seemed there are those who rebelled; they would become angry. And they tried to attack those workers who were giving the message in this end time. But nothing could hinder it. God is going to have a people. God is going to give to the world a demonstration in this last hour such as the world has never known before. Those men and women are of all walks of life. Degrees will mean nothing.

I saw these workers as they were going over the face of the earth. When one would seem to stumble and fall, another would come and pick him up. There were no big "I" and little "you." But every mountain was brought low and every valley was exalted, and they seemed to have one thing in common: there was a divine love—a divine love that seemed to flow forth from these people as they went together, as they worked together, as they lived together; it was the most glorious thing that I have ever known. Jesus Christ was the theme of their life. Is Jesus the theme of your life today? Does He mean everything to you?

They continued, and it seemed the days went by—as I stood and beheld his sight, I could only cry, and sometimes I laughed—it was so wonderful. These people went throughout the face of the whole earth bringing forth in this last end time.

And as I watched from the very heaven itself, there were times when great deluges of this liquid light seemed to fall upon great congregations. And that congregation would lift up their hands and seemingly praise God for hours and even days, as the Spirit of God came upon them. God said, *"I will pour out of my Spirit upon all flesh."* And that is exactly the thing that God was doing. And to every man and to every woman who received this power and the anointing of God (the miracles of God), there was no ending to it.

We have talked about miracles; we have talked about signs and wonders; but I could not help but weep as I read again this morning—at four o'clock this morning—I read again the letter from our native worker, from the superintendent of the church of God, who wrote the letter and told of this native worker. That is only the evidence of the beginning for one man. A "do-nothing," a "nobody," an "unheard-of," who would go and stretch forth his hand and say, "In the name of the Lord Jesus Christ, I command life to come into your body." I dropped to my knees and began to pray again, and I said, "Lord, I know that this thing is coming to pass, and I believe it is coming soon."

And then again, as these people were going about the face of the earth, a great persecution seemed to come from every end of the earth.

Suddenly, there was another great loud clap of thunder that seemed to resound around the world. And I heard again the voice—the voice that seemed to speak, "Now, this is My people; this is My beloved bride."

And when the voice spoke, I looked upon the earth, and I could see the lakes and mountains. The graves were opened, and people from all over the world—the saints of all ages—seemed to be rising. As they arose from the graves, suddenly all these people came from every direction—from the east and the west, from the north and the south—and they seemed to be forming again this gigantic body. As the dead in Christ seemed to be rising first, I could hardly comprehend it. It was so marvelous, so far beyond anything I could ever dream or think of. But, as this body suddenly began to form and take shape again, it took shape again in the form of this mighty giant. But this time, it was different: it was arrayed in the most beautiful, gorgeous white—its garments were without spot or wrinkle as this body began to form. And the people of all ages seemed to be gathering into this body. And slowly, slowly, as it began to form up into the very heavens, suddenly, from the heavens above, the Lord Jesus came—became the *Head*. And I heard another clap of thunder, which said, "This is My beloved bride for whom I have waited. She will come forth, even tried by fire; this is she that I have loved from the beginning of time."

As I watched, my eyes suddenly turned to the far north, and I saw seeming destruction. Men and women in anguish and crying out, and buildings in destruction. Then I heard again the fourth voice, which said, "Now is My wrath being poured out upon the face of the earth." From the ends of the whole world, the wrath of God seemed to be poured out, and it seemed that there were great vials of God's wrath being poured out upon the face of the earth. I can remember it as though it happened a moment ago. I shook and trembled as I beheld the awful sight of seeing the cities and whole nations going down into destruction. I could hear the weeping and the wailing. I could hear the people crying. They seemed to cry as they went into caves, but the caves and the mountains opened up. They leaped into water, but the water would not drown them. There was nothing that seemingly could destroy them. They were wanting to take their life, but they could not take it.

Then again I turned my eyes unto this glorious sight—this body arrayed in the beautiful, white shining garment. Slowly, slowly, it began to lift from the earth. And as it did, I awoke.

The sight that I had beheld—I had seen the end-time ministry, the last hour.

Again on July 27, at two thirty in the morning, the same revelation—the same vision—came again exactly as it had before.

My life has been changed. I realize that we are living in that end time, for all over the world, God is anointing men and women with this ministry. It will not be doctrine. It will not be churchianity; but it is going to be Jesus Christ. They will give forth the Word of the

Lord and are going to say—I heard it so many times in the vision—"According to my word, it shall be done."

Oh people, listen to me. "According to my word. It shall be done." We are going to be clothed with power and anointing from God. We won't have to preach sermons. We won't have to have persons heckle you in public. We won't have to depend on man, nor will we be denominational echoes; but we will have the power of the living God. We will fear no man but will go in the name of the Lord of Hosts.

8

From Here to Eternity

Be patient therefore, brethren, unto the coming of the Lord. Behold, the husbandman waiteth for the precious fruit of the earth, and hath long patience for it, until he receive the early and latter rain.
—James 5:7

Many people believe that we are in the lull before the storm. While some expect that the coming of the Lord will be preceded by a great falling away—"*Because iniquity shall abound, the love of many shall wax cold*"[57]—most Pentecostals are looking instead for a great last-days revival that will sweep the gospel to every nook and cranny of the earth, just as it is described as doing in the vision given to Tommy Hicks. We will probably see both: a great divide forming between believers and nonbelievers, so that differences are evident, and the final choice—making a clear, conscious decision to either accept or reject the gospel. Everyone of accountable age will have a chance to hear and decide for himself whether Jesus Christ is Lord and Savior, raised from the dead by the Father. This is the work of our day and our time. As we said in the beginning, God is not through with us yet.

Unfortunately, the talk of end-times prophecy has had many people looking for what you might call the "spiritual ejection button."

57. Matthew 24:12.

It is as if we are flying around in the most powerfully equipped aircraft, doing incredible stunts and acrobatics every Sunday morning, but when an old WWI biplane of the devil flies onto our radar, we are not ready for attack. Instead, we are shouting, "Lord, rapture us!" We see world events and look for deliverance *from* the earth rather than letting it inspire us to offer deliverance *to* the earth. We are looking for our own escape instead of making sure that when that escape finally becomes accessible, we save as many people with us as possible.

It doesn't take great spiritual discernment to see that the great giant in Tommy Hicks' vision that turns into thousands of people who spread throughout the earth is the church—not a church, not a denomination, and not a nation, but the entire body of Christ spread throughout the earth.

It doesn't take great spiritual discernment to see that the great giant in Tommy Hicks' vision that turns into thousands of people who spread throughout the earth is the church—not a church, not a denomination, and not a nation, but the entire body of Christ spread throughout the earth. Christ, the Head of that giant, enters the picture to stretch forth His hands to save and to endue believers with power, yet many pull back from Him rather than embrace His gift. This prophecy is for all of us in our time. Will we be among those who embrace the call of God on our lives and accept His power to fulfill it? Or will we be among those who pull back from Christ's hands reaching out to us?

We must follow the same steps as David du Plessis to fulfill the prophecy given to him of we desire to see Tommy Hicks's vision fulfilled in our own lives. We must meditate upon, pray over, and ponder the vision. We must see how the vision aligns with Scripture and then follow that pattern, taking heed how we behave and what we teach. We must follow God with all of our hearts and obey immediately when He tells us to do something. We must lift up Christ in all that we say and do. We must stir up the gifts within us for the profit of all. We must walk in faithfulness and humility, as well as love and forgiveness. And we must give ourselves wholly to that vision and calling so that we may accomplish all that God has for us to accomplish—fighting the good fight, finishing the race, keeping the faith. Then, when God finally does hit the "rapture button" to bring us home, we will go with many, many new friends who will remember for eternity what we shared with them.

It is our hope that, through this book, you have learned a few important things, one of which is the significance that prophecy can have and how we should follow it to fulfill the will of God. Another is the necessity of judging prophecy to make sure you are following the truth and not being deceived. Last, and perhaps most important, is that we all have a part in prophecy, and, while God will supernaturally and sovereignly open doors for us to fulfill His will, it is up to us to go through those doors. Clearly, the rewards are for those who will go through, and the regret will be for those who pull back and do not.

All indications are that God is in the process of gathering His body on the earth for a final assault, and the greatest revival of all time is in the very near future. It is our prayer that you will take your place in it, as God directs you. We hope that this book helps you to find the position God has prepared for you *for such a time as this*. God's best!

Part III

Collected Sermons of Smith Wigglesworth, David du Plessis, and Tommy Hicks

9

"The Gift of Prophecy"—Smith Wigglesworth

(Note: This sermon by Smith Wigglesworth is the only one recorded in which he spoke specifically on the gift of prophecy.)[58]

In 1 Corinthians 12:10, speaking of the diversities of gifts by the same Spirit, Paul wrote, *"To another prophecy."* We see the importance of this gift from 1 Corinthians 14:1, where we are told to *"follow after charity, and desire spiritual gifts, but rather that ye may prophesy."* We see also that *"he that prophesieth speaketh unto men to edification, and exhortation, and comfort."*[59] How important it is, then, that we should have this gift in manifestation in the church in order that the saints might be built up and made strong and receive the comfort of God. But with this, as with all other gifts, we should see that it is operated by the Spirit's power and brought forth in the unction of the Spirit so that everyone who hears prophecy, as it is brought forth by the Spirit of God, will know that it is God who is bringing forth the message that is for the edification of those who hear. It is the Spirit of God who takes the deep things of God and

58. This sermon is taken from Smith Wigglesworth, *Ever Increasing Faith* (Springfield, MO: Gospel Publishing House, 1924, 1971), 153–159. Used by permission. All rights reserved.
59. 1 Corinthians 14:3.

reveals them, and it is He who unctionizes the prophet to give forth the revelation of the things of God.

Utterance in prophecy has a real lifting power and gives real light on the truth to those who hear. Prophecy is never a mind reflection; it is something far deeper than this. By means of prophecy, we receive the mind of the Lord; and as we receive these blessed, fresh utterances through the Spirit of the Lord, the whole assembly is lifted into the realm of the spiritual. Our hearts and minds and whole bodies receive a quickening through the Spirit-given word. As the Spirit brings forth prophecy, we find there is healing and salvation and power. For this reason, it is one of the gifts that we ought to covet.

Utterance in prophecy has a real lifting power and gives real light on the truth to those who hear. Prophecy is never a mind reflection; it is something far deeper than this.

While we appreciate true prophecy, we must not forget that the Scriptures warn us in no uncertain manner concerning what is false. In 1 John 4:1, we are told,

> *Beloved, believe not every spirit, but try the spirits whether they are of God: because many false prophets are gone out into the world.*

And John tells us that we can tell the difference between the true and the false:

> Hereby know ye the Spirit of God: Every spirit that confesseth that Jesus Christ is come in the flesh is God: and every spirit that confesseth not that Jesus Christ is come in the flesh is not of God: but this is that spirit of antichrist, whereof ye have heard that it should come.[60]

60. This is a slight paraphrase of 1 John 4:2–3.

There are voices that seem like prophecy. Some people have fallen into terrible darkness and bondage through listening to these counterfeits of the true gift of prophecy. True prophecy is always Christ-exalting, magnifying the Son of God, exalting the blood of Jesus Christ, encouraging the saints to praise and worship the true God. False prophecy deals with things that do not edify and is designed to puff up its hearers and to lead them into error.

Many picture Satan as a great, ugly monster with great ears, eyes, and a tail, but the Scriptures give us no such picture of him. He was a being of great beauty whose heart became lifted up. He manifests himself everywhere today as an angel of light. He is full of pride; and if you don't watch, he will try to make you think you are somebody. This is the weakness of most preachers and most men—the idea of being somebody!

There are none of us who are anything; and the more we know we are nothing, the more God can make us a channel of His power. May the dear Lord save us from the things that cause us to be proud—they are the devil's traps. True prophecy will show you that Christ is all in all and that you are in yourself less than nothing and vanity. False prophecy will not magnify Christ but will make you think that, after all, you are going to be some great one. You may be sure that such is inspired by "the chief of the sons of pride."

There are none of us who are anything; and the more we know we are nothing, the more God can make us a channel of His power.

I want to warn you against the foolishness of listening for voices. Look in the Bible. Here we have the voices of God, who at sundry times and in diverse manners spoke in times past to the fathers through the prophets and has in these last days spoken to us by His Son.[61] Don't run away with anything else. If you hear the voice of God, it will be in line with the Scriptures of truth given in

61. See Hebrews 1:1–2.

the inspired Word. In Revelation 22:18–19, we see the danger of attempting to add or take from the prophecy of this Book. True prophecy, as it comes forth in the power of the Spirit of God, will neither take from nor add to the Scriptures but will intensify and quicken what has already been given to us of God. The Holy Spirit will bring to our remembrance all the things that Jesus said and did. True prophecy will bring forth both new and old things out of the Scriptures of truth and will make them living and powerful to us.

Some may ask, "If we have the Scriptures, why do we need prophecy?" The Scriptures themselves answer this question. God has said that in the last days He will pour out His Spirit upon all flesh, *"and your sons and your daughters shall prophesy."*[62] The Lord knew that in these last days, prophecy would be a real means of blessing in us, and that is why we can count on Him giving us, by means of the Spirit, through His servants and His handmaids, true prophetic messages.

I was at a meeting in Scotland and came in touch with two young women who were in a great state of excitement. These two girls were telegraph operators who were precious young women, having received the baptism of the Spirit. They both longed to be missionaries. But, whatever our spiritual state is, we are subject to temptations. An evil power came to one to these young women and said, "If you will obey me, I will make you one of the most wonderful missionaries that ever went out." This was just the devil or one of his agents acting as an angel of light. One of these young women was captured immediately, and she became so excited that her sister saw there was something wrong and asked the superintendent to allow them to be free for a time.

As she went into a room, Satan, endeavoring to imitate the Spirit of God, manifested himself in a voice and led this young woman to believe that the missionary enterprise would be unfolded that night

62. Acts 2:17.

if she would obey. This evil spirit said, "Don't tell anybody but your sister." I reckon that everything of God can be told to everybody. If you cannot preach what you live, your life is wrong. Someday it will be told from the housetops. Don't think you will get out of it. What is pure comes to the light; he who does what is true comes to the light, that his deeds may be made manifest, that they are wrought in God.[63]

The evil power went on to say to this girl, "You go to the railroad station tonight, and there will be a train coming at 7:32. Buy a ticket for yourself and your sister. Then you will have six pence left. You will find a woman in a carriage dressed as a nurse, and opposite her will be a gentleman who has all the money you need." She bought her ticket and had just six pence left. The first thing came right. Next, the train came in at exactly 7:32. But the next thing did not come. They ran from the top to the bottom of that railroad train before it moved out, and nothing turned out as they had been told. As soon as the train moved out, the same voice came and said, "Over on the other platform." All that night, until 9:30, these two young women were rushed from platform to platform. As soon as it was 9:30, this same evil power said, "Now that I know you will obey me, I will make you the greatest missionaries." Always something big! They might have known it was all wrong. This evil power said, "This gentleman will take you to a certain bank at a certain corner in Glasgow, where he will put all that money in for you." Banks are not open at that time of night in Glasgow. If she had gone to the street this evil spirit mentioned, there probably would not have been a bank there. All they needed was a little common sense, and they would have seen that it was not the Lord. If you have your heart open for these kinds of voices, you will soon get into a trap. We must always remember that there are many evil spirits in the world.

Were these two people delivered? Yes, after much travail with God, they were completely delivered. Their eyes were opened to see

63. See John 3:21.

that this thing was not from God but from the devil. Those two sisters are now laboring for the Lord in China and doing a blessed work for Him. If you do get into error on these lines, praise God, there is a way out. I praise God that He will break us down until all pride leaves us.

Paul wrote at the command of the Lord,

> *Let the prophets speak two or three, and let the others judge. If anything be revealed to another that sitteth by, let the first hold his peace. For ye may all prophesy one by one, that all may learn, and all may be comforted.* (1 Corinthians 14:29–31)

If you are not humble enough to allow your prophecy to be judged, it is as surely wrong as you are wrong. Prophecy has to be judged. A meeting such as this one that Paul suggested would certainly be the greatest meeting you ever had. Praise God, the tide will rise to this. It will all come into perfect order when the church is bathed and lost in the great ideal of only glorifying Jesus. Then things will come to pass that will be worthwhile.

> *If you are not humble enough to allow your prophecy to be judged, it is as surely wrong as you are wrong. Prophecy has to be judged.*

Coupled with prophecy, you will have goodness, the fruit of the Spirit. They are holy men who spoke in prophecy in days of old as the Holy Spirit prompted them, and so today the prophet who can be trusted is a man that is full of goodness—that goodness that is the fruit of the Spirit. But when he gets out of this position and depends on his own personality, he is in danger of being puffed up and becoming an instrument for the enemy.

I knew some people who had a wonderful farm, very productive, in a very good neighborhood. They listened to voices telling them to sell everything and go to Africa. These voices so unhinged them that they scarcely had time to sell out. They sold their property at a ridiculous price. The same voices told them of a certain ship they were to sail on, but when they got to the port, they found there wasn't a ship by that name. The difficulty was to get them not to believe these false voices. They said perhaps it was the mind of the Lord to give them another ship, and the voice soon gave them the name of another ship. When they reached Africa, they knew no language that was spoken there. But the voice did not let them stop. They had to come back, brokenhearted, shaken through, and having lost all confidence in everything. If these people had had sense to go to some men of God who were filled with the Spirit and seek their counsel, they would soon have been persuaded that these voices were not from God. But listening to these voices always brings about a spiritual pride that makes a man or woman think that they are superior to their brethren and that they are above taking the counsel of men whom they think are not so filled with the Spirit as they are. If you hear any voices that make you think that you are superior to those God has put in the church to rule the church, watch out; that is surely the devil.

We read in the Revelation that the testimony of Jesus is the spirit of prophecy.[64] You will find that true prophetic utterance always exalts the Lamb of God.

No prophetic touch is any good unless there is fire in it. I never expect to be used by God until the fire burns. I feel that if I ever speak, it must be by the Spirit. At the same time, remember that the prophet must prophesy according to the measure of faith. If you rise up in your weakness—but rise up in love because you want to honor God—and just begin, you will find the presence of the Lord upon you. Act in faith, and the Lord will meet you.

May God take us on and on into this glorious fact of faith, that we may be so directed by the Holy Spirit that God will work through us on the line of the miraculous and on the lines of prophecy, where

64. See Revelation 19:10.

we will always know that it is no longer we but He who is working through us, bringing forth that which is in His own divine good pleasure.

10

"The Three Types of Prophecy"—Smith Wigglesworth

(Note: The following transcription is from teaching sessions by Rev. Smith Wigglesworth during the summer of 1927 to Bible students at Aimee Semple McPherson's Angelus Temple. The material included here was from two sessions when Rev. Wigglesworth was discussing spiritual gifts sometime that July. Excerpted here are his lectures specifically discussing prophecy.)[65]

I want you to understand clearly that there are three classes of prophecy. Get it in your heart, because Paul desired that we all prophesy.[66]

1. *The prophecy that is the testimony of the saved person.* We find this prophecy described in Revelation 19:10:

> *And I fell at his feet to worship him. And he said unto me, See thou do it not: I am thy fellowservant, and of thy brethren that have the testimony of Jesus: worship God: for the testimony of Jesus is the spirit of prophecy.*

65. These lectures are taken from Smith Wigglesworth, *Smith Wigglesworth Speaks to Students of the Bible*, complied by Roberts Liardon (Tulsa, OK: Albury Publishing, 1998), 51–57, 63–66.
66. See 1 Corinthians 14:5.

This is the same prophecy that Paul spoke about in 1 Corinthians 14:1:

> *Follow after charity, and desire spiritual gifts, but rather that ye may prophesy.*

Here prophecy is chosen as more important than charity or other gifts. Think about that: Prophecy is to be chosen and desired above faith, hope, charity—above all other the gifts. The greatest among them all is prophecy.

Why prophecy? Because prophecy by the power of the Spirit is the only power that saves humanity. We are told in the Word of God that the gospel that is brought through in prophecy has power to bring immortality and light. Immortality is that which abides forever. Light is that which opens the understanding of your heart. Light, immortality, is by the gospel.

Prophecy is to be coveted above all things, and every person has to have it. Now, every person may have gifts, but there are very few that do. But everybody has prophecy.

Now, from that same reference in Revelation, let us see what prophecy is and how it comes forth. *"I fell at his feet...."* *"I"*? Who is it? I would like all the people who have been so foolish—I call it foolishness because there is nothing that makes you so foolish as to turn aside from the Word of God. If ever you want to be a fool, turn aside from the Word of God, and you will find yourself in a fool's paradise.

The one speaking here is a man who has been in the earth. Lots of people are foolishly led by the devil to believe that they are asleep in the grave, absolutely contrary to the Word of God. Don't you know that even the body that you have, if you live to the Lord, comes itself to be put off and another put on, because you cannot go into heaven with your body? This man has been in the earth in the body and is now in heaven in the spirit, and he wants you to hear what he has to say.

> *I am thy fellowservant, and of thy brethren that have the testimony of Jesus...for the testimony of Jesus is the spirit of prophecy.*

What is the testimony of Jesus? I am saved. What the world wants to know today is how they can be saved. Testify that you are saved. Your knees may knock together; you may be trembling as you do it; but, when you get it out, you enter into the spirit of prophecy. And before you know where you are, you are saying things that the Spirit is saying.

Now you come to a point where you say, "Is it the Holy Spirit?"

No, indeed.

What is it, then?

It is the Spirit of Jesus that you got when you were saved. There are thousands of people who never have received the Holy Spirit that have this wonderful spirit of prophecy. People are being saved all over by the testimony of people who have never been baptized in the Holy Spirit, but they have the spirit of prophecy.

John Wesley was moved by the power of God and created revivals all over the world. After the people were saved, they testified.

If you cease from testifying, you will be sorry when the accounts are made. You are the power of salvation to people. Testify wherever you are.

Message Through Tongues and Interpretation

> You have not chosen Me, but I have chosen you and ordained you that you should go forth, your feet shod with the preparation of the gospel of peace. What lovely feet!

> What lovely desire! A desire in your heart because you are saved, to get everybody saved. The spirit of prophecy!

You must all preach from this morning. Every one of you must be a preacher. You have a prophecy that has come from heaven to change you from vile inward corruption, transport your human, evil nature, put within you a spirit of testimony, because you know, where once you were dead, behold, you are alive!

Message Through Tongues and Interpretation

> Live in the place where the Lord thy God moveth thee, not to go from house to house nor to speak from person to person, but where the Lord directeth thee, for He has the person which is in need of truth waiting for watering with your water can.

Oh, how the Lord wants to cheer you today! Do not forget that you are ambassadors for Christ. Don't forget you are in the place now where the prophets have a chance.

The Lord can bring you into a great place of splendor. He has His hand upon you. Whatever you do, covet to be holy, seek to be clean, so that you might always bear about in your body not only the dying of the Lord but the life of the resurrection of the Lord.

Message Through Tongues and Interpretation

> Lift up your hands and never be feeble, for the Lord has said, "Lift thy holy hands." Don't be afraid of coming into the treasury, of making thine hands clean, for they that bear the vessels of the Lord have to be only unto the Lord. So that Lord is bringing thee to this great place of His pavilion, that He may clothe thee upon with the Spirit, that thy water shall not fail. He shall give thee water and seed for thy ministry, for remember, it is the same water and it is

the same Sower. So don't forget, beloved, you are coworkers together with Him, and your ministry in the Lord is not to be in vain. See to it that you live so that your seed is well watered.

Now, that is one class of prophecy. General Booth knew it. He got the vision as clear as anything from Wesley. The greatest revival that has ever swept the earth yet that we remember is the revival the Salvation Army brought. I know they have lost the glory, the power, and the unction because they turned to philanthropic positions. But that does not mean we have to lose it.

God revealed Himself to Booth, every person was saved that would testify, and He moved the people that were saved, drunkards and harlots, into the streets to prophesy in the Spirit of Jesus.

This is the prophecy that you all have when you are saved. The spirit of prophecy is the testimony that you are saved by the blood of the Lamb.

2. *Every preacher that lives in unction has the second class of prophecy.* You will find that I mostly speak in prophecy. Why? Well, it has pleased the Lord to bring me into this order so that I do not come to the platform with thought, not thoughts of what I am saying.

I want you to know another thing: I never say what I think. It is very much below a prophet of the Lord to begin to speak to the people what he thinks. *The prophet must always say what he knows, because the people he is speaking to are the ones that have to think it out.* But he is in the place of knowledge. The Holy Spirit takes the thoughts of Jesus and fills him with life divine until he speaks divine utterances, until he knows.

Sometimes I speak ever so much, never take any thought at all concerning what I am speaking, but it flows out like rivers—prophecy of divine power.

It is very important and very essential that the person who preaches should live in prophetic utterance.

It is very important and very essential that the person who preaches should live in prophetic utterance. Then, a preacher should never be lamentable in his divine position. He is standing before the people as a chosen one of God. He does not have in any way to bring his position in anything less than it is the Word of God that is speaking, and there he is to be clothed with holiness like a garment of salvation.

Oh, this is true! The Spirit of the Lord is upon me now. I know it. I feel it. It is moving me. It chastens me. It is bringing me to a place where I know, if you listen, you will be blessed. The blessing of the Lord is upon you. Hear, for the Spirit speaks to you.

This prophecy as the Spirit gives forth, the illumination of truth by the Word of Life, the Holy Spirit having the chief position in the place, taking words, acts, everything, until He stands there complete, He is the oracle of God, speaking words absolutely according as if the Lord were here saying them.

3. *The gift of prophecy.* There is another prophecy that I trust many of you people will have because it is the gift of prophecy.

What are the other two? The other two prophecies are divine inspiration, Holy Spirit utterances.

Every person, in a very remarkable way by the Spirit of Jesus, can feel burnings and movings, chastening and thrillings. It is wonderful. All you have to do is begin, and you cannot stop.

There was something done on the cross that is truly wonderful. Don't you know you were made every whit whole. You were made holy. You were made a saint. You were absolutely cleansed from all unrighteousness. The new birth is a revelation of God in the soul. You are made His forever when you are saved by His power. No one can estimate the new birth. It is beyond all human power to estimate. The new birth is larger than our human capacities. And, thank God, we have touches that make us on fire.

Now, the next, divine prophecy is a gift. There are people who, like Isaiah, have this prophecy. Isaiah was so filled with this prophecy—"Behold, a Son is given."[67]

Definite, personal truth knowledge. It took five hundred years to bring it to pass, but there it was, definitely declared: *"And the government shall be upon his shoulder: and his name shall be called Wonderful, Counsellor, The mighty God, The everlasting Father."*[68]

Oh, hallelujah! All the way down, you will find you get the prophecy, so distinct. You will see Isaiah filled with prophetic utterances. Begin with Genesis and go right through, and you will find the golden or the scarlet thread right through all the prophecies, "He is coming. He is coming! He is on the way. He will surely come!"

The angels sang, the Babe was born, "And they called his name Jesus, for He saves His people from sinning." Prophecy fulfilled! "He shall in a manger lay; He should die on the cross; as Moses lifted up the serpent in the wilderness; so must the Son of Man be lifted up."

Ah, beloved, God can give you prophecy that will fulfill the past to a perfect degree, chapter, verse.

He is coming, glory to God! The saints shall be awakened, the prophecy will appear. People will say, "Yes, He is coming. We all know He is coming!"

And He will come!

(Continued in the next session partway through.)

---

67. See Isaiah 9:6.
68. Ibid.

We didn't exactly finish the word of prophecy yesterday morning, because I wanted you to see that there is a great deal of trouble through prophecy. There always has been. So I want you to guard this gift.

There are three classes of prophecy. The first position of prophecy everyone has, every newborn soul. Through the new birth unto righteousness, God has given an unction of the Spirit, a real unction of the Spirit of Christ. When we were saved, we felt we wanted everybody to be saved. That has to be continuous. The whole world can be regenerated by the spirit of prophecy as we testify to our saving position in Christ.

The next type of prophecy is the preacher who delivers in prophetic utterances. My natural makeup is not full, but my supernatural makeup is an overflowing full. I depend upon an overflowing full, that you may get something out of it, that you may overflow full.

I now turn to the prophecy that is the most wonderful of all prophecy, and yet the most dangerous. What you have to watch is this—the same in the gift of tongues, just the same in the gift of healings, just the same in prophecy—you have to watch this: Because the gift has been received and the people [have] been blessed through the gift, you are never to use this gift without the power of the Spirit bringing into you a great thirst and longing to do it. It would be a serious thing for me to speak in tongues at any moment just because of the gift, without the unction of the Spirit, and it would fall to nothing.

All gifts are of no account at all unless they are brought forth by the Giver of the gifts, and the Holy Spirit is the One who gives the nine gifts.

All gifts are of no account at all unless they are brought forth by the Giver of the gifts, and the Holy Spirit is the One who gives the nine gifts. And He has unction, fire, zeal, and expression until those who hear are moved, because when the Lord speaks, it changes and moves the natural, because it is supernatural. Supernatural always changes natural.

Prophecy is lovely, because it makes the body very full of expressions of joy. It is lovely, for people all like to hear it. It is lovely when it is the Spirit moving.

You be careful now when the people are very pleased to hear you prophesy. Prophecy is like tongues; no man is to have advantage in a meeting that speaks and speaks and speaks and speaks in tongues. This is not an advantage. Advantage is that, when the Spirit is upon you, you will speak in tongues, and you will close down the moment when you know you are at the end. What spoils it is people going on and on, and the hearers are tired of it because they want something that God can bring in and move quickly.

Don't you think you will be heard by your much speaking, either by tongues or by praying or anything. You are not heard because of your much speaking. You are heard because you are definite. All your spiritual abilities are going to be acceptable with others as you learn how to obey the Spirit and never take advantage because you are in the place.

Another thing you have to learn: People rush up and down sometimes and say to you, "Oh, I was obliged to do that! I was obliged to jump up and to do that. I was obliged to do that, and that, and that."

Don't believe them. It isn't true. There never was a man in the world, as long as he was in the body, that didn't have power over the Spirit. And so when people rush to you and say they are obliged to do this, that, and the other, don't you believe it. What should you believe? You have to believe that *when the Spirit is manifested in the order it should be, it will have three things with it: comfort, consolation, and edification.*[69]

---

69. See 1 Corinthians 14:3.

If any of you find I do not speak by the Spirit of God and bring the Scriptures only, that which God desires, you meet me at the door and tell me. I have declared that this shall be my constant purpose. I have declared that as long as I live I shall never exaggerate. Exaggeration is lying. *What God wants is a people that is full of truth.* I want God to so have you that your word will be the bond. If ever you say a thing, the people will be able to believe. You have said it, and you will do it.

When the unction is upon you, when the power of God is manifested through you, one thing that will be accomplished by prophecy is comfort.

When the unction is upon you, when the power of God is manifested through you, one thing that will be accomplished by prophecy is comfort. The Holy Spirit can so have you in prophecy that all the people will be comforted.

But if you get away from that prophecy because you begin and the people are delighted, go on until you come out with your human words, you will lead people astray. People have been led to buy houses, to do all sorts of silly things, because of people who did not obey the Lord but brought in some human prophecy.

If anybody ever comes to you with human prophecy, say, "I know God, and without God gives me, I won't move."[70]

Don't you be deluded by anybody. You can tell what is from the Lord. The Word of God distinctly says, "Do not despise prophecy."[71] Whatever you do, do not despise it. But in the next words, you are told to "judge all things."[72] Say, "Well now, if that is from the Lord, I will see if it is of the Word of God." And you will have clear revelation as to whether it is the word of the Lord.

70. Meaning, "Unless I know God is the one giving this word to me, I won't act upon it."
71. See 1 Thessalonians 5:20.
72. See 1 Thessalonians 5:21.

This is the day that we need comforting, and the power of the Spirit can comfort you and send you away from these meetings knowing that you have been in the presence of God and heard the Word of God.

11

"Gather the Wheat—Burn the Chaff"—David du Plessis

(Note: This message was preached 1947 at the opening of the First World Pentecostal Conference in Zurich, Switzerland, and subsequently in many churches, Bible schools, and conventions throughout Europe and North America.)[73]

In the beginning of this century, when the Holy Spirit was being poured upon Holiness groups almost simultaneously everywhere in the world, the first reaction from the established churches was a strong objection to the noise and seeming disorder in the prayer meetings. This was so entirely different from the quiet, almost over-regulated, church services, that many religious leaders declared the revival was a wildfire movement. The Pentecostal preachers, on the other hand, declared boldly that they had received a baptism of the Holy Spirit and fire.

Now, after fifty years, this phenomenal revival has spread to all nations in all countries of the world, and Pentecostal churches

73. This sermon is taken from David J. du Plessis, *The Spirit Bade Me Go* (Plainfield, NJ: Logos International, 1970), 99–106. Used by permission. All rights reserved.

have been established. It is nothing unusual, in these days, to hear preachers declare from Pentecostal platforms that many manifestations in some meetings are due to fanaticism, if not wildfire. In the beginning, we were very fond of considering enthusiastic young converts just filled with the Holy Spirit and full of shout and song as being "on fire." Such on-fire believers of today look upon the older and experienced Pentecostals as having become lukewarm and cold because they do not demonstrate reactions such as they had when they first came into the Pentecostal experience.

Was the exuberance of the new convert wrong? Has the experienced believer cooled off or backslidden during recent years? Let us look into these questions. First, let us study the grass roots of what is known as the Pentecostal experience.

Just before the birth of Christ, the people sat in darkness. For generations, there had been no prophet. There remained only a ceremonial religion. Malachi, the last of the prophets, had said:

> *Behold, I will send my messenger, and he shall prepare the way before me: and the Lord, whom ye seek, shall suddenly come to his temple, even the messenger of the covenant, whom ye delight in: behold, he shall come, saith the* Lord *of hosts. But who may abide the day of his coming? and who shall stand when he appeareth? for he is like a refiner's fire, and like fullers' soap: and he shall sit as a refiner and purifier of silver....* (Malachi 3:1–3)

The land of Judea is stirred once again. A prophet appears on the scene. He ignores the temple and the synagogues and preaches on the banks of Jordan. He calls everyone to repentance and pronounces judgment upon the self-righteous. To the latter, he says:

> *Think not to say within yourselves, We have Abraham to our father: for I say unto you, that God is able of these stones to raise up children unto Abraham. And now also the ax is laid*

unto the root of the trees: therefore every tree which bringeth not forth good fruit is hewn down, and cast into the fire.
(Matthew 3:9–10)

Note here the "fire of judgment."

Suddenly, the great prophet turns to the repentant sinners and says:

I indeed baptize you with water unto repentance: but he that cometh after me is mightier than I, whose shoes I am not worthy to bear: he shall baptize you with the Holy Ghost, and with fire [note that this is not "judgment fire" but rather the "refiner's fire"]: whose fan is in his hand, and he will thoroughly purge his floor, and gather his wheat into the garner; but he will burn up the chaff with unquenchable fire. (Matthew 3:11–12)

From the words of the prophet, it seems clear that a baptism of fire would be needed to burn up the chaff when the wheat had been separated from it. The fan is in the hand of the Baptizer. He will purge His floor; He will burn up the chaff. It is also clear that both the Baptizer and the baptism in the Holy Spirit would be as real as John and his baptism in water were. He declares that the kingdom of heaven is at hand and then tells of the mighty King and the glorious blessings to be expected from His hand.

When Jesus came upon the scene, He said:

I will pray the Father, and he shall give you another Comforter, that he may abide with you for ever....But the Comforter, which is the Holy Ghost, whom the Father will send in my name, he shall teach you all things...he shall testify of me.
(John 14:16, 26; 15:26)

In confirming the prophecy of John about the coming of the Holy Spirit, the Lord Jesus emphasized the fact that He will be a

Comforter. Small wonder, then, that those who receive the baptism of the Holy Spirit become so exuberant with joy. Such persons are not "on fire," as was often said, but they are "filled with the Holy Ghost." The consequence is that they produce the same manifestations as the first disciples did on the day of Pentecost. It was on that very day that the religious world began to register objections and accuse the Spirit-filled believers of being filled with new wine. It is no different today. We have the same Holy Spirit, the same baptism, the same manifestations—tongues and apparent drunkenness—and the same objections and accusations.

What was Peter's defense? *"This is that"*![74] What? The fulfillment of the prophecy of Joel: *"In the last days, saith God, I will pour out of my Spirit...your sons and your daughters shall prophesy."*[75] But the prophet says nothing about speaking in tongues and acting like drunken people. Yes, this is the beginning of that. From now on, He will lead into all truth. Prophecy will follow.

Now, pardon a little of my personal testimony. Some years ago, I passed through one of those spiritual crises that come into the experience of every growing Christian. I was hungry for a deeper experience with God. I was tired of the repetition of spiritual manifestations that did not seem to bring edification to anyone but myself. I wanted to see the manifestation of the Holy Spirit in operation in my life. One night, in desperation, I decided I would not go to sleep until the Lord had given me some very definite guidance. My prayer was, "Lord, where must I go from here? This is not the end of the road, for I have always declared that the baptism in the Holy Spirit was only the beginning and not the end of a closer walk with God." After midnight, He spoke to me clearly and said that I needed a baptism of fire. Immediately, I concluded that because I was no longer as demonstrative as before and did not shout and speak in tongues as loud and long as I did twenty-five years before, I must have lost the fire. I prayed with all my heart

74. Acts 2:16.
75. Acts 2:17.

that He would baptize me with fire, whatever that might mean. The yielding of that night brought profound things into my life, and my ministry did change. I was a happy man, but I had no desire to shout and sing and leap before the Lord as I did in my younger days. I was ready to do so, but it seemed the Lord did not require that from me.

After enjoying the wonderful, deeper life for a few weeks, I discovered that some very cherished things in my life were dropping off. Some of my brethren seemed to misunderstand me. My best friends seemed most unsympathetic. I felt so lonely at times that life became a burden. Again I sought guidance and light from the Lord, for I feared to trust in man.

One Sunday morning, very early, I made my way into a wilderness and lay myself in the dust before the Lord. I felt as if twenty-five years of Christian life and years of ministry were all in vain. Nothing remained, and I was just an utter failure. As I wept before the Lord and humbled myself, a peace that passes understanding suddenly came over my soul. I lay almost as dead. Then it seemed someone was speaking to me in very gentle tones. He said, "I am answering your prayer. It is the baptism of fire." I complained that I did not feel "on fire" at all.

Then, He said, "But the fire does not bring joy. It burns, it devours, it reduces, it purges. The Holy Spirit gives comfort and joy, but the fire cleanses and sanctifies. I am removing the chaff from your life." Once again, I began to weep and asked the Lord to show me what sin there was still in my life. Very gently I heard Him say, "Chaff is not sin. I am not removing tares but chaff. Chaff is good, and indeed it is essential in order to obtain wheat. When the chaff is removed, you will see the wheat."

I heard Him say, "Chaff is not sin. I am not removing tares but chaff. Chaff is good, and indeed it is essential in order to obtain wheat. When the chaff is removed, you will see the wheat."

I shall never forget those wonderful moments in His presence. It seemed that He brought me to a green field. I recognized it as growing wheat. Then I found myself in a barn and saw bags of wheat. It seemed as if I were listening to a conversation between two people. As the one passed his hands through the wheat in the bag, he told the other that this was clean rich wheat. We left the barn and looked on the field again. "Beautiful green grass," said the one. "No! Beautiful growing wheat," said the other. "How can that be? This does not look nearly like the things in the bag." "Yet it is true...this is that, and that is this. If you will leave this to develop, it will produce wheat such as in the bag, but when you plant what is in the bag, it dies and lives again to produce what you see here."

Again I saw a wheat field. Now it had grown higher, and in the gentle breezes, the heads of ripening wheat waved to and fro. I heard one say, "Soon it will be ripe, and then it must be gathered to the floor, where the chaff can be separated from the wheat. The chaff has served its purpose, and if it is not removed soon, it will destroy the wheat crop. If, however, you remove the chaff before the wheat is ripe, you will have no crop either. Just one more rain, and there will be enough moisture to ripen this wonderful field." I stood amazed. There I saw tall stalks of straw, and the ears of wheat were only six inches long. Why, even the wheat kernels were surrounded and covered with chaff. What a process the gathering and threshing is. A threshing floor looks anything but orderly. In the end, however, the winnowing fan separates wheat and chaff, and order is restored.

After this revelation, I was left alone with my thoughts. What could it all mean? Then I remembered my earliest Pentecostal experience. How often I had wondered whether all the noise and manifestation in a prayer meeting was produced by the power of the Holy Spirit. But why should people want to act so strangely and get great blessing out of it? At such times, I heard a still small voice say to me, "This is that." I was satisfied, because that was the answer Peter gave on the day of Pentecost. Later on, I saw and heard and personally experienced very clear manifestations of the gifts of the Holy Spirit. Instead of tongues only, there followed the interpretation of tongues. Instead of only tongues and interpretation, there followed prophecy. In the sermons of my brethren and in my own messages, I began to discern moments when preaching was prophecy, moments when there was the word of wisdom, and moments when there was a word of knowledge.

How did all this come about? Where did it begin? This is how I see it now. First stammering lips, then new tongues, then interpretation of tongues, then prophecy, then words of wisdom and knowledge, all by the same Spirit.

> *So is the kingdom of God, as if a man should cast seed into the ground; and should sleep, and rise night and day, and the seed should spring and grow up, he knoweth not how. For the earth bringeth forth fruit of herself; first the blade, then the ear, after that the full corn in the ear. But when the fruit is brought forth, immediately he putteth in the sickle, because the harvest is come.* (Mark 4:26–29)

Just as the growing wheat on the field responds to every little breeze, so young Christians filled with the Holy Spirit will respond to the breezes of heaven. Just sing a chorus over again, and they begin to rejoice and wave their hands. I have noticed that the converts of very sedate and calm preachers are just as emotional as the converts of the shouting and running evangelist. Some of these sedate old preachers were, in fact, very demonstrative in their early Christian experience. The precious brother or sister who now brings such wonderful messages in tongues and interpretation or in prophecy was once as noisy as some of the worst shouters among the young converts. Most mature Christians have found that it took years before they learned to yield to the Holy Spirit so that He might use their lips to prophesy rather than to speak in tongues. Paul thought that five words that are understood are worth more than ten thousand words in a tongue that cannot be understood. But then, there are usually several feet of chaff before the ear of grain comes. There might be years of seemingly useless manifestations before we ripen into faith that will produce prophecy.[76]

If you refuse to let the Lord fan the needless demonstrations from your life and you cling to the initial reactions only, you will never have the ripened fruit of the gifts of the Spirit.

In our Pentecostal churches today, there seem to be two extremes. The apostle had a word of warning for both. To those who object so fervently against noise and disorder, he said, *"Quench not the Spirit."*[77] To those who want nothing but these disorderly manifestations, he said, *"Despise not prophesyings."*[78] If you refuse to have seemingly needless manifestations—chaff, as you may think—you will never have the gifts of prophecy. If you refuse to let the Lord fan the needless demonstrations from your life and you cling to the initial reactions only, you will never have the ripened fruit of the gifts of the Spirit. The apostle was quite aware of this, and so he wrote that wonderful chapter 14 in the first epistle to the Corinthians. This chapter will never quench the Spirit, but it will regulate the growth of the saints in the church.

Have you ever watched a modern threshing machine that has taken the place of the old-fashioned threshing floor? There is a lot of shaking and trembling and noise. On the one side, there is a mountain of chaff, and on the other just a few bags of wheat. What a lot of chaff to produce so little wheat. Put a match in the chaff, and what remains will be nothing, compared to the wheat in the bags.

76. See Romans 12:6.
77. 1 Thessalonians 5:19.
78. 1 Thessalonians 5:20.

Let us get the correct perspective of spiritual things. Be tolerant and thank God for the growing wheat. Be in no hurry to separate the chaff. Remember, the fan is in His hand. On the other hand, we must not be satisfied with a good old shouting camp meeting. Let us honor the Holy Spirit and give Him opportunities to speak to us, for He came not only to comfort us but to lead us into all truth. If we only make noise in our meetings, we will not hear His voice. Let us have the waving grain when the breezes blow, and thank God for it, but do not judge those who have no part in such demonstration, for not even a hurricane will make a bag of wheat wave. We need wheat for new fields, and we need growing fields for more wheat.

There is nothing that can ever take the place of the Holy Spirit in the church. Let us pray for a greater outpouring than ever; and remember, when the floods come, it will not keep to our well-prepared channels, but it will overflow and most probably cause chaos in our regular programs.

In recent years, I have become more and more burdened because I find a strong tendency among older pastors to take the fan in their hands. I am told by some that they no longer allow tongues in prayer in public meetings. They will not have the "camp-meeting style" of singing and shouting and clapping of hands in their churches. I find many churches where there is never any sign of a truly Pentecostal manifestation. They are afraid of manifestations in the "flesh," and so they conduct the whole meeting "in the flesh," but decently and in order. In such meetings, I feel as I do in a home where there are no children, no babies that cry. Everybody behaves perfectly, but it is so dull and so monotonous. Babies and children always do the unexpected. What are we doing with our spiritual babies? Where do we train them? In the basement? Will they ever learn that they belong to the family...the church?

Then again, I have come to other churches that give me concern. There is no recognition of wheat, and there is a premium of chaff—loud talking, shouting, and singing for an hour. Everybody is speaking in tongues, but there is never any interpretation. It is Pentecostal indeed, but still in the chaff stage—babies crying, children tumbling. It looks bad when adults act like children. Some must come to maturity. There must be tongues with interpretation of tongues, and there must be prophecy and other manifestations. In such churches, I plead that they invite the Baptizer to bring in His fan and then give them a baptism of fire. I have seen too many shouting Christians go to sleep when the Word is preached. They live on "milk" and choke on the "meat" of the Word.

> *For when for the time ye ought to be teachers, ye have need that one teach you again which be the first principles of the oracles of God; and are become such as have need of milk, and not of strong meat. For every one that useth milk unskilled in the word of righteousness: for he is a babe. But strong meat belongeth to them that are of full age, even those who by reason of use have their senses exercised to discern both good and evil.*
>
> (Hebrews 5:12–14)

12

"A Pentecostal in Ecumenical Circles"—David du Plessis

(Note: This lecture was given at Highleigh, Hoddesdon, Herts, England.)[79]

What is a "Pentecostalist"? It is someone who can testify to having enjoyed the very same experience as that which the apostles of our Lord had on the day of Pentecost, according to Acts 2. I hear the term "Pentecostal" more frequently than "Pentecostalist," so I shall make use of the former term in this message.

What is the Pentecostal movement? On the whole, this term includes all those societies and movements or missions that teach and preach that all Christians should receive the baptism in the Holy Spirit as they did on the day of Pentecost, according to Acts 2:4, with the evidence of speaking with other tongues as the Spirit gives utterance. This seemed to be the "proof" of the baptism in the Spirit that the apostles recognized.

In Acts 10:45–46, Luke said, "*On the Gentiles also was poured out the gift of the Holy Ghost.* ***For*** *they heard them speak with tongues,*

79. This sermon is taken from David J. du Plessis, *The Spirit Bade Me Go* (Plainfield, NJ: Logos International, 1970), 9–20. Used by permission. All rights reserved.

and magnify God."[80] The phenomenon of tongues appeared again in Bible schools and in missions and prayer groups at the turn of the century. Today there are scores of societies, often referred to as sects, that have tens of thousands of churches in every part of the world, with millions of members who have actually received the baptism in the Holy Spirit and have spoken with tongues. The entire Pentecostal movement has about ten million adherents and is one of the fastest-growing fundamentally Christian movements in the world.

The entire Pentecostal movement has about ten million adherents and is one of the fastest-growing fundamentally Christian movements in the world.

In 1900, when this new revival began, there was a battle against it at once. The opposition was not so much against the teaching of the baptism in the Spirit as against the speaking with tongues. All the historic churches rejected this vehemently. It was considered rank heresy to claim to speak with tongues by the Spirit. But *now,* after fifty years, the climate has changed. Today, the same phenomenon of tongues is being witnessed in many of the historic churches: Last year, American papers carried headlines like these: "Strange Manifestations—Speaking with Tongues Amazing Churches Again" and "Staid Episcopal Clergyman Speaking with Tongues." This partly gives you the reason why a radical Pentecostal like myself has become involved in ecumenical activities.

I was born in South Africa and came from French Huguenot stock. Then I was born again in 1916. Actually, I was a little white heathen saved by the life and ministry of black Christians. My father was building a home for missionaries in Basotuland, and that was when and where it happened.

The impact upon my young life was not from the preaching of the gospel but rather the miracle of the change that I saw in the lives

80. Emphasis added.

of illiterate pagans around me. What Christ did for them and what the Holy Spirit did through them deeply impressed me. I knew that I had nothing of that. I realized that it was not literacy that changed them, for they had none. I knew their testimonies were not intellectual, for there was too much evidence of the supernatural. I knew it was divine, for many of these people had been steeped in witchcraft and demonism, and now they were completely delivered and changed into saints who loved Jesus so much that they would die for Him.

In 1918, when we had moved back to the Union of South Africa, I was in high school. Then I began to seek the same blessing, and the Lord graciously met me and baptized me as He had baptized the saints in New Testament churches, according to the book of Acts. So, I am an old-timer in Pentecost, and I haven't seen great miracles during the past forty-three years.

I now realize that what the churches need today is this blessing. Recently, Dr. Carl Henry, editor of *Christianity Today,* wrote, "In twentieth-century Christianity, the Holy Spirit is still a *displaced person*. Liberal theology exiled this divine person from the life of the church in favor of simply divine 'function.' Recently a distinguished theologian told me: 'When Christianity lost the Holy Spirit as the divine person who leads into all truth, the Spirit was soon misunderstood (by idealistic philosophy) only as Mind, indeed as human mind. The ability of distinguishing spirits was lost.' How right he was. Whenever the church makes the Spirit of God a refugee, the church—not the Spirit—becomes the vagabond."

Almost everywhere I go, I hear of the lack of the Holy Spirit and His life in the churches. People have lost interest in church services because there is so little relevancy to their spiritual problems to be found there. Man's spirit hungers after God. Only the Holy Spirit is the water of life that will quench the thirst of the human soul.

Then I think of what Dr. John A. MacKay, immediate past president of both Princeton Theological Seminary and the Presbyterian

Alliance, recently told a Presbyterian convention: “A crudely emotional approach to religion is preferable to religious formalism that is purely aesthetic and orderly and lacking dynamic power.” He said further: “One of our serious troubles in the church today is that it has become legitimate to be emotional in anything but religion. The need is for something that will summon one’s whole enthusiasm. The moment the church becomes completely programized and depersonalized, it becomes a monument to God’s memory and not an instrument of His living power.”

Statements like these from ecclesiastical leaders and theologians disturb me, because these are confessions that they realize something is wrong with the church. Something is lacking, but confession is not enough; there must be an acceptance of God’s remedy—a Pentecostal revival in the churches.

Something is lacking, but confession is not enough; there must be an acceptance of God’s remedy—a Pentecostal revival in the churches.

I began preaching at a very youthful age. In those days, there was much preaching against the Pentecostals. I used to listen to Dutch Reformed ministers preach against us and call us false prophets standing on street corners. Then I would promptly go back to the street corner and preach against “these blind leaders of the blind.” How we attacked one another. But I thought it was my duty to “contend for the faith.”

My parents had been turned out of the Dutch Reformed Church, and I had great bitterness in my heart for this injustice to people who lived like saints. Yes, I could quote Scripture that would sometimes seem to cool off the heat of my bitterness. I remember one day I was challenged to “speak with tongues.” I said, “I certainly will not.” “But why not?” Quick on the trigger, I said, “Because the Bible says: ‘Cast not your pearls before swine.’” How good I felt that

I could call them "swine." Later I discovered this was not "in the Spirit" but very much in the flesh. I was still so carnal.

Do I hear you say, "But the Spirit should make you perfect"? Yes, He does. But He does it by manifesting Himself through imperfect people. The church at Corinth was one of the most carnal churches, yet they had more manifestations than others. If you ask me why, I would say, "Because the Holy Spirit sought so desperately to wake them up. He is as faithful to plead with us to repent as to convict us of our faults."

In 1947, the first World Conference of Pentecostal churches was called in Zurich, Switzerland. They gathered from many countries, and I came from South Africa. The conference took no real decision for further conferences, so in 1948, the leading brethren asked me to convene the next conference in 1949 in Paris, France. Thus, up to 1958, I served most of the time in what some now call the capacity of ecumenical secretary of the movement.

I have just returned from the sixth Pentecostal World Conference in Jerusalem. How good it was to be there without administrative responsibilities. The Israeli government had loaned their great new convention hall to us for the weekend of May 19–21. I shall never forget that great Communion service on Sunday morning, when about 3,000 delegates and visitors from forty countries sat down at the table of the Lord.

Let me explain. Even though we have a world conference now, the Pentecostal movement had never been developed or propagated from one center, unless that center is heaven. I do not think there will ever be one central world headquarters. This revival "just happened" in most countries and has become indigenous almost everywhere. There is no man who can claim to have been the founder of this movement. It is the work of the Holy Spirit. When we first met, in 1947, there developed better understanding, more recognition, and more appreciation of one another as leaders. We were all happy to recognize that the Lord was bringing His people together. My personal ambition was to see the entire movement united on the basis of recognition rather than by organization. We do have a lot of division on issues of doctrine and church government, just like many other great Protestant movements.

When the Protestants came together in 1948 to form the World Council of Churches at the first Assembly in Amsterdam, I heard it said, "This is the work of the devil. This is an attempt to form a super-church." I was greatly puzzled, for I could not believe that God would allow the Protestant world to become an instrument of the devil. Why should Pentecostal unity be of the Lord and Protestant unity be of the devil? Was it not the Lord who was moving us to unity in both movements? These questions kept troubling me until I began to pray earnestly about *His* purposes.

In 1951, the Lord spoke to me and clearly told me to go and witness to the leaders of the World Council of Churches. In my prayers, I said, "Lord, I have preached so much against them. What do I say to them now? They will not listen to me. Their churches have put our people out of their fellowship. That is why we have now a separate Pentecostal movement. The churches were not willing to listen to the testimony of those who speak with tongues." But the Lord kept telling me to go and witness to them.

Besides speaking with tongues, there was another very important doctrine and practice that the churches had rejected—namely, divine healing. In my estimation, Mr. James Moor Hickson was the man God used to really set the churches right on this matter. Pentecostals could not do it, although they were preaching the message and praying for the sick in almost every meeting in those days. Until this

Besides speaking with tongues, there was another very important doctrine and practice that the churches had rejected—namely, divine healing.

day, I consider Mr. Hickson as God's great apostle to restore to the world the reality of divine healing.

Finally I decided to obey the Lord. I asked my wife to prepare an early breakfast because I was going to New York that day. She asked me what I was going to do. I explained that the Lord had commissioned me to go and witness to the leaders of the World Council of Churches. I can still hear her saying, "What will you try next?" I replied, "I am not trying anything. I am just obeying the Lord. But I will be back by lunch." I expected to be dismissed so quickly that I would not want to stay in New York very long. At that time, I lived close by, in Connecticut.

When the offices on Fifth Avenue opened, I was there. I announced myself and made sure there was no mistake about who and what I was—a Pentecostal, and one of the worst, actually the world secretary. In the train on my way in, I had decided to make things so hot that those I spoke to would have no trouble in knowing what I had to say, and I expected them to object and reject. But the hotter I made it, the better my friends seemed to like it. This one friend kept saying, "Go on, tell us some more. We have been waiting for a fellow like you to come and talk to us." This continued until lunchtime. I apologized for taking so much of their time. He said, "Do you eat lunch?" When I said I did, he invited me to go with him. He would pay for the lunch if I would keep on talking. He took me back to the office and invited others in and made me repeat a whole lot of these things that I thought they did not want to hear. I was kept busy until closing time that afternoon. That was my first encounter with the WCC.

In 1952, I was invited to come to the International Missionary Council, extended Assembly, at Willingen, Germany. This was my first experience as a Pentecostal in an ecumenical convention. I checked in for three days, thinking I could not live on cold shoulder for more than that. But when I arrived on the conference floor during coffee break, Dr. John A. MacKay, who was president of the

IMC, took me by my arm and went down the line, introducing me as his great Pentecostal friend. There was no mistake. I was not evangelical or fundamental but distinctly *Pentecostal*.

The next day, a speaker complained that Christianity had become so institutionalized that it would be a blessing if some of these institutions burned down. Dr. MacKay then informed them that while they were worrying about their institutions, he would like to call on a friend who came from a movement that had encircled the world with missions in less than half a century, and that without institutions. He said to me: "Come and tell us in two five-minute periods *why* and *how* the Pentecostals accomplished so much in so short a time."

I assured the gathering that I did not come to boast about any achievements of the Pentecostals, but in answer to the questions, I could only say, "The reason why Pentecostals have been so successful in missions is because they are Pentecostal." Then I noticed a few frowns, and I continued, "Gentlemen, I did not say it is because we speak with tongues, for if that was all we had from the experience of the baptism in the Holy Spirit, we would have been a forgotten issue long ago. However, Jesus said: 'Ye shall receive power,' and that is the secret of our success. Untrained and sometimes illiterate people went forth without boards or institutions to help them, simply guided by the Holy Spirit, who confirmed their preaching with 'signs following.' They established beachheads for Christianity in the most unlikely and difficult places, where others had even failed.

"Now for the questions: How did you do it? I would say, 'In the old-fashioned apostolic way of witnessing—each one tell one.' It was when the church in Jerusalem was scattered abroad (all except the apostles) that they went everywhere preaching the Word. Today we scatter the apostles, and the church members have nothing to say. The Pentecostal movement started out as a witnessing community. However, you cannot teach people to be witnesses; they become witnesses when they have an experience of something. The courts of our day will not accept a 'prompted' witness. A good Pentecostal witness is one who can tell how he got saved and healed and baptized in the Holy Spirit. Such a testimony is more powerful than a sermon on salvation and healing and the Holy Spirit."

I stayed at Willingen for the full period of eleven days. I had interviews, by their request, with 110 of the 210 delegates. This then placed me in touch with many of the ecumenical leaders and officers of the World Council of Churches.

In 1954, I was invited by Dr. Visser 't Hooft, the WCC secretary, to go to the Second Assembly of Evanston. When I asked him what he wanted me to do, he told me that I should do exactly what I did at Willingen—just witness and talk to as many as possible about my Pentecostal experiences. When I suggested that I might be mistaken for a "schismatic," trying to cause division among brethren, he assured me that he had been convinced that I had no such intentions, for he had not found anyone in my contacts to whom I had suggested that they should leave their church. I agreed to go, and it was arranged that I could serve on the staff, in the press section. This gave me just the opportunities I needed to talk to archbishops, bishops, professors, and principals and presidents of institutions. Sometimes I kept going until after midnight.

I thought this would be the end of my ecumenical outreach. But in 1956, I was invited to a retreat in Connecticut to speak to a group of ecumenical leaders on the American front. That was one of my greatest experiences in this ministry.

Twenty-four ecumenical leaders were comfortably seated around me. They had invited me to bring them the truth about the Pentecostal experience and the Pentecostal movement. I was asked to be devastatingly frank. This very request caused me to seek the face of the Lord, to be sure that I would meet these friends just as Jesus would have done if He had been there in person. I could remember days when I had wished I could have set my eyes upon such men to denounce their theology and pray the judgment of God upon them for what I considered their heresies and false doctrines. Here was such an opportunity, and they said, "Be devastatingly frank." I prayed, "Lord, what would *You* have me to do?"

That morning something happened to me. After a few introductory words, I suddenly felt a warm glow come over me. I knew this was the Holy Spirit taking over, but what was He doing to me? Instead of the old harsh spirit of criticism and condemnation in my heart, I now felt such love and compassion for these ecclesiastical leaders that I would rather have died for them than pass sentence upon them. All at once, I knew that the Holy Spirit was in control, and I was beside myself and yet sober as a judge.[81] Thank God, from that day on, I knew what it meant to minister along the *"more excellent way."*[82] This indeed is the technique of the Holy Spirit.

For seventy-five minutes, I poured from my heart all that the Spirit gave me. Never have I known a more attentive audience. If things were happening to me, I realized the same Spirit was doing things to my listeners. This was very evident when the time came for questions and answers. There was an unaffected desire to know all about the gifts and ministries of the Holy Spirit. The promise of Jesus was made so real to me: *"But when they shall lead you,...take no thought beforehand what ye shall speak, neither do ye premeditate: but whatsoever shall be given you in that hour, that speak ye: for* ***it is not ye that speak, but the Holy Ghost.****"*[83]

Then there came a question that presented an opportunity to be devastatingly frank, but I had no desire to belittle or criticize or hurt anyone. Silently I prayed. The question was: "Please tell us what is the difference between you and us. We quote the same Scriptures as you do, and yet, when you say those words, they sound

81. See 2 Corinthians 5:13.
82. 1 Corinthians 12:31.
83. Mark 13:11 (emphasis added).

so different. We say the same things that you do, but there seems to be a deeper implication in what you say. You have said nothing with which we want to differ, and yet there seems to be a distinct difference somewhere." What was I to say? What was the truth? The Spirit came to my rescue, and I said, "Gentlemen, comparisons are odious, and I do not wish to injure anyone's feelings or hurt your pride. But the truth as I see it is this: You have the truth on *ice*, and I have it on *fire*."

"That is too deep for me; please explain," said one.

"Gentlemen, we have been dealing with the meat of the Word," I answered, "so please allow me to illustrate what I mean. I live in Dallas, Texas, where it can become very hot. We have a deep freeze to preserve food in bulk. When meat is at a reasonable price level, we buy half a steer. Thus, I know there is the very best grade of Texas steer T-bone steak in that freezer. If any of you were to visit my home, I would like to serve you such a steak. Suppose I take it out of the freezer and place it on a plate before you; could you eat it? Of course not. It is just a frozen chunk of iced meat. But we could discuss it. We could even record the facts. It weighs about twelve ounces. It contains so many calories. There are several vitamins in it. We know the butcher who sold it. We may know the ranch that raised the steer. We may know the pedigree of the steer and its age, and so forth. Then we could go the other way and decide, if you eat it, it will satisfy your hunger. It will add to your weight, and so forth. But after half an hour of good 'beef discussion,' it is still there, and we are still hungry. Our minds have been fed with information but the beef was not enjoyed.

"Now what shall we do? Something needs to be done to that meat to make it edible, and make our facts real. I give it to my wife. Without inquiring about our collected facts and information about the steak, she places it on *fire*. Within a few minutes the atmosphere in the house changes, and everyone knows something is cooking.

My little boy comes in and shouts, 'Mom, something smells good, and I am starving.' We are all served a nice hot steak off the fire, and we say, 'That just hits the spot.' Is my little boy going to get sick because he does not know all the facts about the beef?

"You know, gentlemen," I continued, "here we have the elements of a good Pentecostal meeting. There is an atmosphere. Everyone knows something is happening. The old alcoholic that sits there does not have to listen to the theology of saving grace; he is not told the theology or doctrine of regeneration. He gets the 'hot gospel' stated in facts—God loves you. God will save you. Ask and it shall be given you. Seek and ye shall find. Do it now. Jesus is here to meet you. He will give you the water of life, and you will never thirst again—and the sinner accepts the invitation. In a few minutes, he rises from his knees and *knows* something has happened to him. In his life, something has hit the spot. He is now a changed man. There will be plenty of time to teach him the doctrine and theology of his experience later on. After all, I submit there was a Pentecostal experience of the baptism in the Holy Spirit in the lives of the apostles before they ever developed or framed the doctrine and the theology. They had experience and no doctrine. Today most people have doctrine and no experience.

> *The church does not need better theologies, but rather men full of faith and of the Holy Spirit.*

"My friends," I said, "if you will take the great truths of the gospel out of your theological deep freezers and get them on the fire of the Holy Spirit, your churches will yet turn the world upside down. The church does not need better theologies, but rather men full of faith and of the Holy Spirit[84]—men who will say, '*Our sufficiency is of God; who also hath made us able ministers of the new testament; not of the letter, but of the spirit: for the letter killeth, but the spirit giveth life.*'[85]"

84. See Acts 6:5.
85. 2 Corinthians 3:5–6.

After this, one of those dear men said, "Why did I not meet someone like you many years ago? I realized my ministry was not a success, but I could not find the reason for my failure. Now I discover my spiritual temperature was not right. I lacked the power of the Holy Spirit."

> The Scripture is a key to itself. Besides, we have the Holy Spirit to open it to us....God is His own interpreter. We fail to understand the Scriptures, because we seldom accept His help. This, I feel assured, is the reason why we are so often in ignorance. It is not that the truth sought for is not in the Word, but that through lack of communion with Him who gave the Word, we have not enough of His mind to apprehend His meaning, even where He has fully expressed it.
>
> —Andrew Jukes, in *The Law of Offerings*

My next thrilling experience was the 18th Council of the Presbyterian World Alliance in Sao Paulo, Brazil, during 1959. I attended as a Pentecostal Fraternal delegate with some 600 other delegates from 56 countries representing 46 million Calvinists. When the president of the Council, Dr. John A. MacKay, introduced me, he remarked, "Whatever else history may have to say about our friend, this fact will surely be recorded. This is the first confessional body that has extended recognition to the Pentecostal movement as a sound Christian body. The records will also show that Princeton Seminary was the first institution to recognize this by inviting our friend as missions lecturer."

In my heart, I thought: *How wonderful. Calvinist churches were the first to disfellowship members with a Pentecostal experience at the turn of the century. Now fifty years later, they recognize this as the work of the Holy Spirit.* I find this is what is happening all over the world. The climate in the churches is changing rapidly.

During the last three years, I have had the privilege of lecturing at many institutions besides Princeton Seminary. I have been to Yale Divinity, Union Theological Seminary in New York, Southern Methodist University in Dallas, Colgate Rochester School of Divinity, Fuller Seminary in Pasadena, British Columbia University in Vancouver, the Ecumenical Institutes in Switzerland and America, and other centers. After this visit to England and Holland, I went to the Second Latin American Evangelical Conference in Lima, Peru, in August.

In the past, I have not given much publicity to these activities because I fear that publicity often kills good things. Besides, I did not want to embarrass my friends who were so kind to me, and I certainly did not want to exploit my privileges to any personal advantage. Recently, a group of Episcopal ministers in America asked me who sponsored me in this work and what my position was now in the Pentecostal movement. I had to explain that this was a faith venture. No one hired me, and no one can fire me. I have resigned from every position I held, and so I have become just a great "has been" insofar as positions are concerned. I am a goodwill ambassador for Christ. I travel as the Lord provides through His people, and He takes care of my family, too.

Now in conclusion, let me say what a great honor and privilege it was to be one of the speakers at the recent meeting of the Commission of Faith and Order at St. Andrews, Scotland. There I made contact with some of the Roman Catholic observers. So, I have actually had an opportunity to learn all about the ecumenical movement, which is greater than the World Council of Churches or the Roman Catholic Church and all the orthodox churches together. From Pentecostalism to Catholicism there are "winds of change" blowing. I pray that these may become again the "mighty rushing winds" of the day of Pentecost.

13

"Seventy Times Seven"—David du Plessis

(Author's note from Simple and Profound *by David du Plessis: If the author had but one message to bring, it would be on the importance of forgiveness. Early in life, he learned how it could change everything, and he has been a living example of its power ever since.)*[86]

Where Did Forgiveness Begin for You?

In the beginning, I was not a forgiving person. I knew firsthand about the fights between the Pentecostals and the Protestants, because I was in the thick of them. For instance, when I went to a Dutch Reformed church and heard the minister attack our movement and call it false and an evil thing because it was causing disturbances in the Protestant churches, I sat there and thought, Why is he a Christian? Jesus caused disturbances in the synagogue and the temple.

I *was* concerned about the prayer that Jesus taught His disciples—"Forgive us as we forgive others"—but I assumed it applied

86. This sermon is taken from David du Plessis, *Simple and Profound* (Orleans, MA: Paraclete, 1986), 119–126. Used by permission. All rights reserved.

only to the body of believers that I happened to be in. We were born again, and others were not, and so I considered them a mission field and not a Christian body. I had lost sight of the truth: that churches were still churches, and they still had Christ. I had taken the Pentecostal attitude of "Come ye out from among them," because *they* had been pushing *us* out. They had been expelling us, and to us it was more respectable to come out than to be pushed out.

As I grew older, I stopped fighting, but I still had not forgiven the churches. And then I came to realize that my "word of wisdom," my "word of knowledge," and all my preaching were not helping anyone, because I was not preaching in love to the people. I had not learned to forgive and love. If you forgive, then you have to substitute love for old feeling.

Then one day, the Lord said to me: *What Smith Wigglesworth told you is soon to come about.*

"But, Lord, he told me to go to the old-line denominations, and they're dead."

I never arranged for funerals. You had better raise the dead.

"Lord, they're enemies."

Then love them.

"How can I love people that I don't agree with?"

Forgive them.

"I can't justify them."

I never gave any child of Mine authority to justify anyone. I gave you full authority to forgive them. That's all you have.

So I forgave the Protestants for all they had done to the poor Pentecostals, and I forgave the Catholics for all they had done to the poor Protestants. Then the Pentecostals wanted to know who had given me the authority to do that, and so I had to forgive the Pentecostals!

I live by forgiveness. And I love by forgiveness, because they can do anything they want to; I just forgive them.

Is Forgiveness Only for Christians, or Can It Work in the World?

I once asked a judge who was a Christian and had been on the bench for forty years: "Were you usually able to settle a case, when you had the necessary witnesses and evidence?"

He thought for a moment before answering. "You know, when I look back, I realize I almost never really settled a case. I only helped them to come to an agreement to stop litigation, and to stop spending money."

"But, you know," I replied, "God Himself abandoned the law and on Calvary introduced forgiveness. That is God's new way. The Law—no law—could save anybody, or help anybody. But forgiveness is always successful."

He shook his head sadly. "I dare not speak of forgiveness in court. I'm a judge, and on the bench I've got to judge." And then he smiled. "But I can invite the disputing parties into my chambers, and there is where I can really settle cases by forgiveness."

I nodded. "Thank you! You have helped me to see it in relation to our own situation. What a pity that the church, instead of preaching forgiveness, became judges or prosecutors." I sighed. "In fact, that was my own job for years. I thought it was my duty to prosecute everybody, to get them straightened out, according to the law. Why, I made even the Sermon on the Mount a law: 'You've got to live according to the Sermon on the Mount—that's what Jesus taught!' But I had forgotten that Jesus did not teach that in order to make it a law; He taught that it was the consequences of a new birth." And I thanked the judge again for further clarifying my perspective.

Must We Forgive Everyone? For Everything?

Yes, even the Nazis for the Holocaust. I said this once, a long time ago, and Loren Cunningham heard me. He was just a boy then, twelve years old, but he took it and decided that he would follow my example. (He never dreamed that he would have to follow me through expulsion and all the rest.) Accompanied by teams of young people with his Youth With a Mission, Loren had made a specialty of evangelizing at Olympics, and in 1972, he acquired a beautiful castle in Germany for his headquarters at the Munich Olympics. He had some of his best YWAM people with him, strong teams with a lot of field experience and good preparation—but they were making no headway; they could not win a single convert.

In despair, they called a prayer meeting and wept before the Lord. And Loren, sensing that the Lord held him personally responsible, cried out, "Lord, speak to me: what is wrong? We had success in Mexico, at the Olympics there; we've had success everywhere. You have blessed us; You have provided the facilities and all the equipment we need. And yet here we cannot move. Why?"

And then he heard the Lord: *You have not forgiven Hitler.*

"But Lord, Hitler is dead."

Not in your mind. You still hold all Germans responsible for the Holocaust. All Germans did not agree with Hitler, but you do not know that. Unless you forgive them, you will never help them to recover.

Loren told the others what the Lord had revealed to him, and together they forgave Hitler, and everyone else involved. Immediately things changed. God blessed their ministry mightily, opening doors that had previously been closed to them and enabling them to win many converts.

Loren told me that the lesson changed the Youth With a Mission approach from then on. "You can be sure that, now, before any mission, we ask God to search our hearts for anything, known or unknown, we might be holding against those we seek to help."

Must Forgiveness, Then, Be Always Unconditional?

"Walk in love," the apostle wrote—I am not crippled; I must *walk*. And the walk must be in love. This is where the Lord helped me, when He said, *You cannot love people if you have not first completely, unconditionally, forgiven them. You have too many conditions.*

That unconditional forgiveness did not come in the beginning. (Thank God, He didn't tell me everything at once; I would have given up!) It was revealed step-by-step, and the latest was when He said: *On Calvary, Jesus made no conditions. He simply said, "Father, forgive them, for they know not what they do." Your forgiveness is still: "If they do this, if they do that." You still expect some sign of repentance, and then you'll forgive. You must forgive people, no matter how they behave, no matter whether you think they are worthy. You just forgive. And if you forgive them, you can love them. And if you love them, you can beat any enemy; but you will never win your enemies if you don't love them.*

How do we make enemies? By finding fault with each other. By hurting each other in speech and in our thoughts. So, I had to learn to "walk in love, as Christ loved us and gave Himself for us, a sacrifice unto God."[87] That is why I like the verse: *"Hereby perceive we the*

87. See Ephesians 5:2.

love of God, because he has laid down his life for us: and we ought to lay down our lives for the brethren."[88] That kind of love is unconditional.

When I began to see this, things began to happen that I'd never seen before. I had no way of knowing what the effect would be, but I could see that Jesus on the cross had granted unconditional forgiveness to the Jews who shouted, "Crucify Him!" and to the Romans, Jews, and Gentiles—that means all humanity. He had forgiven once and for all, and that was sealed with His blood.

He was doing this, even as His blood poured out, and that is why we now say He cleanses us. True, but the cleansing comes when we accept His unconditional forgiveness. Our own forgiveness must be unconditional, too; we must not forgive people just because they do something that pleases us. We must forgive our enemies.

An example: Here comes a man called Saul of Tarsus, wreaking havoc with the church, which he found not in the temple but from house to house. Stephen, who had been chosen a deacon, had become a powerful evangelist, and Saul said that if this young fellow carries on like this, he'll convert all Israel. We must put him out of the way. So he gathered a mob and stoned him, and when Stephen saw the end was coming, he fell to his knees. He saw heaven open, and he saw Christ standing. Christ stood up to welcome him home, but before he went, he said, "Father, lay not this sin to their charge." That was unconditional forgiveness.

And what happened? Jesus had taught that what you bind on earth shall be bound in heaven, and what you liberate on earth shall be liberated in heaven. Here, Stephen liberated Saul of Tarsus, the leader of the mob, from judgment. "Lay not this sin to their charge"—that caused the King of Kings, the Lord of Lords, the Prince of Glory, the Mighty Savior, to come from His throne all the way down to the road to Damascus, to arrest Saul of Tarsus.

88. 1 John 3:16.

He made him His prisoner, and Paul always spoke of himself as a prisoner of Christ.

This example, of the most dangerous enemy of the church who became its champion, gave me the grace and courage to forgive. I don't care how much they fight the charismatic movement or what they do to the Pentecostals, I forgive them. And I have seen some of the greatest fighters of the opposition, even those who said we are of the devil, become champions of the movement. The Lord can change people! In fact, He said to me: *You can turn all your enemies into champions, if you will forgive them so unconditionally that they cannot escape it.*

Does That Explain Your Lapel Pin, "70 × 7"?

Yes, and it helps remind me that forgiveness is a continuing affair. Because the temptation to stop forgiving is always present.

(The message concluded in a note that he would make these pins available free of charge to anyone who wrote to him and asked for one.)

14

"The Message of Deliverance"—Tommy Hicks

(Note: This sermon was preached in 1955 in Argentina.)[89]

It is a great pleasure to see so many people here and to bring a message of deliverance from the Word of God.

Open your Bibles to 2 Corinthians 2:14—"*Now thanks be unto God, which always causeth us to triumph in Jesus Christ, and maketh manifest the savor of his knowledge by us in every place.*" God tells us in this verse that He always causes us to triumph by the knowledge that God gives us in Christ.

In another verse, the apostle Paul says, "I can do all through Christ who lives in me." The first part of the verse we read was, "*Thanks be unto God, which always causeth us to triumph in Jesus Christ.*" For the Christian, there is no defeat. We can overcome every defeat. We can overcome all fear, because Christ lives in our souls. Repeat please: "Christ in me, Christ in me, Christ in me." Now friend, think that Christ lives in you. How can you be defeated? There is no defeat for men and women who walk with the Lord. And God wants you to know that if Christ is in you, you have

89. This sermon is taken from Tommy Hicks, *It's Closing Time, Gentlemen* (Los Angeles: Manifest Deliverance and Worldwide Evangelism, Inc., 1958), 27–35. Used by permission. All rights reserved.

power to rise up over every defeat. God wants you to know that sickness and disease do not belong to you. The sickness and disease could have overcome and defeated you, but when you remember that the living Christ lives in your soul, you can rise up against every defeat. There is no defeat for men and women who remember that Christ lives in them. The sickness and disease cannot have dominion over their bodies; the living Christ lives in them.

The Scripture says, "*Thanks be unto God, which always causeth us to triumph in Jesus Christ.*" How can we be victorious? There is only one way to be victorious, and that is when we possess the knowledge of Christ, when we have the knowledge of the living Christ in us.

The Bible teaches us that we are like a piece of soil. When the soil is worked, one can sow seed in it, and that seed sprouts and grows and gives fruit. We are like a piece of soil. In 1 Corinthians 3:6–9, God says that we are gardens, planted with the Word of God. The word "*husbandry*" should be translated to "field" or "garden." This is wonderful. If you allow the Word of God to be sown in your body, it will grow and give fruit. It will produce 60, 70, or 100 percent. It will produce as much as you will allow it to. Your body will produce results of the Word of God. I want to repeat to you again that the Word of God must be received in your body and you must let it grow. Then it will flow from you—the glory of the Word that has been planted in you.

The reason why some of you are not triumphant, the reason why sickness and disease always defeated you, is because you do not have the Word of God sown in you. If you allow the Word of God to be sown in you, when sickness and disease come against you, you have something to go against the power of sickness and disease. Take the Word, read it, put it into your heart. Say, "It is mine. I proclaim it as mine and allow it to be mine." Continue reading and praying until it is yours. When the Word of God is in your soul, it will answer when sickness and disease come. The triumph of Christ will follow. "*Thanks be unto God, which always causeth us to triumph in Jesus Christ.*"

When you get to know how powerful the Word of God is—oh! David knew something about that. He said in Psalm 119:11, "*Thy word have I hid in mine heart, that I might not sin against thee.*" Take the Word of God and memorize it. Allow it to be a part of you. The more you read, the more you sow. You will find the Word of God will be blood for your body and power for your bones. Friends, the Word of God is the most powerful thing in the world! We don't notice how powerful the Word of God is! There is a Scripture in Hebrews 4:12 that says, "*The word of God is quick, and powerful, and sharper than any twoedged sword.*" When you use the Word of God, what does it do? It breaks everything.

The Word of God Is a Sword

When Satan comes against you, answer him not with your knowledge but with the sweet savor of the Word of God. When you do that, the devil has to go away. The Word of God is a sword. It is something that God has given you to defeat the devil. When you have the Word in your soul, you can use it like a machine gun. You can know so much of the Word of God that you will be like a man with a machine gun who is firing at the enemy. Don't tell the devil what you know, but say what God has said. You can give so much of the Word of God and give it so quickly that the devil must flee away, and yet you can give so little that the devil comes and defeats you. Learn what God has said, and when the devil comes, you will defeat him.

Not Your Knowledge

The reason why some of us fail is because we give our own knowledge in the great sermons we preach. Your knowledge is not the knowledge of God. Use the knowledge of the Word of God, and you will find that the knowledge of the Word of God will cause you to triumph. Those old, dry sermons are so dry that a puff of wind will blow the dust. You must use the Word of God against the devil and you will make him flee. The Bible says, *"Submit yourselves therefore to God. Resist the devil, and he will flee from you."*[90] When the devil comes, you will defeat him. The Word of God will do what God has said it would do. The Bible says that one will chase a thousand, and two put ten thousand to flight.[91] When you use the Word of God against the devil with all your strength, going against him, not in your own strength and power but in the knowledge of Christ, you will be triumphant, and you will find that God is with you.

The Gifts of the Spirit Defined

Someone asked, "Can I use the knowledge of God?" Yes! God has made it possible that every believer in Christ, full of the Holy Spirit, can speak, think, and act like God. But you can only do this when you have the baptism of the Holy Spirit and the nine spiritual gifts that are at the disposition of every man and woman. God has given us nine spiritual gifts. Each one represents the supernatural power of the Word of God. Listen—I am going to name them: a word of knowledge, a word of wisdom, discerning of spirits, faith, healings, miracles, prophecy, tongues, interpretation of tongues.

The nine spiritual gifts are divided into three divisions. The first division is:

The Gifts of Revelation

They are a word of knowledge, a word of wisdom, and discerning of spirits. These gifts only manifest themselves in your life by the power of the Holy Spirit. Notice it does not say "knowledge" or "wisdom" but a "word of knowledge" and a "word of wisdom." Some

---

90. James 4:7.
91. See Deuteronomy 32:30.

are going about, saying, "That man has the gift of knowledge for the great things he is doing." That is not what God means when He says a word of knowledge. The word of knowledge is given while you are under the anointing of the Holy Spirit. God reveals to you a word, or two, or ten, and you speak the words under the inspiration of the Holy Spirit. The same happens with a word of wisdom, which God gives you to do something. Through the word of wisdom, Solomon could take a child, and ask for a knife, and by that wisdom find out who the mother of the child was. These two gifts are given in a "wink of an eye." Listen—the most ignorant man in the world can be filled with the Holy Spirit, and God can make him speak a word of wisdom or a word of knowledge, that could put Einstein, the most highly intellectual man in the world, to confusion. I am so happy that the Word of God says that God takes the most humble and fills him with the Holy Spirit, for the wisdom of the world is foolishness with God. I am so happy that you and I can obtain the wisdom of the Holy Spirit.

The third gift in this section is "discerning of spirits." Some people want to know something about another person and say, "I can discern you did this or that." That is suspiciousness. The gift of discerning of spirits is to know what spirits are in the human body. For example, if a person comes before a man of liberation who has the gift of discerning spirits, the Holy Spirit falls and reveals to him the name of the spirit in that person. He can call him by name and in the name of Jesus tell him to go out, and the spirit will obey his voice.

God wants you to know you can have the gifts of the Holy Spirit if you walk with Him and the Word of God is sown in your soul.

The second division is called:

The Gifts of Power

There are three gifts of power: faith, healing, and miracles. The greatest is faith. A man whose faith is manifested in his life in its fullness can expect healing and miracles to take place. Now, God does not confine this power to preachers. If you will notice again and again, "These signs shall follow them that believe." When faith is manifested in your life, then the gifts of healing and miracles take place automatically. As the *gift of discernment* controls the first two gifts of revelation, so does the *gift of faith* control the other two gifts of power. We could go on and on with this tremendous revelation of the power gifts, but let us come to the next division.

The Gifts of Inspiration

Now, how are the gifts of inspiration manifested? Exactly as the word *inspiration* [implies]. They operate only as you are inspired by God or the Holy Spirit. As you yield yourself to God in the spirit, the gift of inspiration automatically begins to operate in your life. They are known as prophesying, speaking in tongues, and interpretation. There is no other way in which these gifts can operate except as you are inspired by the Holy Spirit. These gifts are found in 1 Corinthians 12:7–11, but listen to this quotation: *"But all these worketh that one and the selfsame Spirit, dividing to every man severally as he will."*[92] Now, that means that it is up to you. Power is a matter of choice. You can have as much power with God as you want.

I want you to know the difference in these gifts. The first is the gift of revelation. How do these gifts come? Through revelation!

The second division is the gift of power. As one exercises faith, the gifts of healings and miracles come forth automatically.

The third division is the gifts of inspiration. The first gift, prophecy, controls speaking in tongues and interpretation.

To sum it all up: If a man has the gift of discernment, he can be assured that the other two gifts will operate in his life. *Faith* controls the gifts of power, and *prophecy* controls the gifts of inspiration.

92. 1 Corinthians 12:11.

I want to read to you 2 Corinthians 2:15: "*For we are unto God a sweet savor of Christ, in them that are saved, and in them that perish.*" What are we? Sweet savor of Christ. Are you a sweet savor for God? Are you sure? Are you sure that you are a sweet savor of God? God says that we are a sweet savor of Christ. Now, I don't know; you say that you are unto God a sweet savor of Christ. There is only one way I can know if you are unto God a sweet savor of Christ, and that is if the Word of God has been sown into you—if the Word of God is living in you. If so, you are unto God a sweet savor of Christ. But I wonder how we smell before God if the Word of God is not sown in us.

God wants you to know that when the Word of God is sown in you, you have the knowledge of God living in you. Here is what happens: I possess the knowledge of God. Do you see why the devil has defeated us? Because we didn't possess the Word living in us. If the Word of God is in you, you will be like a soldier that wins one battle after another. You can use the sword in your hand and say, "Christ guides me to victory!" There is only one way to be triumphant, and that is that the knowledge of God lives in your soul.

Don't you love the Lord tonight? I love Him more than ever before. I will tell you something. If you continue praising the Lord as you do tonight, oh! I want you to shout and praise the Lord! There is nothing as dead as a meeting where not one says "Amen" and does not praise the Lord. Everybody is sitting with a long face. I don't criticize them for it. They don't praise the Lord, because they do not have the Word of God in them. But if you have it in you, when the preacher is preaching, you have a right to shout.

I am happy that the Word of God has life in itself. Read Shakespeare and you will see that it is a dead book, but read the Word of God and you will see that it has life in it.

Make up your mind that you will be filled with the Word of God. Some of us are spiritually so thin that we are only skin and bones. God wants you to be full of His Word; then, you will be sweet savor before God. Do you want to be sweet savor before God? If so, get full of the Word of God and you will have the knowledge of God. And when you have it, He will give you wisdom to use the power that has been given to you.

15

"The Burning Bush"—Tommy Hicks

(Note: This sermon was also delivered in 1955 in Argentina.)[93]

I want to encourage your hearts tonight, so that when you feel the power and the presence of God, it is a sign that you are in touch with God; you can ask Him anything, and He will give you the desire of your heart; it is the moment to release your faith. Do not fear to call unto God in that moment of time; for when you feel the presence of God, that means that you must ask in that same moment, and He will touch your body and soul.

Tonight, I want to read to you [from] the third chapter of Exodus, verses 3 and 4:

> *And Moses said, I will now turn aside, and see this great sight, why the bush is not burnt. And when the* Lord *saw that he turned aside to see, God called unto him out of the midst of the bush, and said, Moses, Moses. And he said, Here am I.*

I want you to notice something in what we have read. First, that God was speaking to Moses, and Moses was alone in the desert.

93. This sermon is taken from Tommy Hicks, *It's Closing Time, Gentlemen* (Los Angeles: Manifest Deliverance and Worldwide Evangelism, Inc., 1958), 102–107.

While Moses was looking after his cattle, suddenly his eyes caught sight of a burning bush. Why did it seem so strange to him? For there were so few of those bushes in that place. I have seen the same place where Moses saw the burning bush, and for many miles, one can't see a single bush. Therefore, it was not surprising that when Moses saw it, he went aside to see it and said: *"I will now turn aside, and see this great sight, why the bush is not burnt."* For how long Moses watched this bush, we don't know, but he must have observed it for some time, because finally he said, *"I will now turn aside, and see this great sight, why the bush is not burnt."* And when he turned, there was something different in it from any other bush that had ever existed on the face of the earth; for God had done something strange with this bush: He had changed the very nature of this bush, so that this bush could hold God and His presence. Think of that—that God had changed the very nature of that bush so that that bush could hold the presence and power of God, for from that bush God began to speak. It must have been very astonishing, for while Moses was watching, he became quite excited, and when he got near the bush, God began to speak to him.

A Seeking God

God had come to the place where He was looking for a man. He had His reasons to seek him, and He found Moses and said to him, "Moses, go and free My people." First, God had people to deliver; second, the time had come for their deliverance. Now God had found the man, and He said, *"Draw not nigh hither: put off thy shoes from off thy feet, for the place whereon thou standest is holy ground."*[94] Moses was observing the burning bush, and his desires were becoming each time greater, for God was in the bush, and His power and His presence could be felt. God wants you to feel His presence! God wants you to feel His power!

94. Exodus 3:5.

What a wonderful story! God descended and entered that bush, and suddenly that bush began to speak. Moses heard the bush, and this is what he thought: *I wish to have what that bush has.*

Friends, listen to me: that is what God wants you to know—that you can have the fire of God; God can speak through you, the same way He can speak through the bush, the same way He can speak through you and me and will cause His fire to come into you.

I can imagine Moses saying, "I want that fire, I want that fire, I want that fire! I want that voice to speak through me. I am meek. I have no power in myself. I want the power that that bush has!" God said to Moses, "I will make you a burning bush." Moses was to become an instrument for God, an instrument in the hands of God to deliver the people that were in slavery. He said to Moses, "My people are in slavery." Notice the commandment that He gave him; He said, "Go and deliver My people." Moses said he could not speak, but God made him know that He would give him power, and he would become a burning bush.

What God Wants You to Know

That is what God wants you to know. In Acts 2:4, we read about the hundred and twenty disciples that were assembled together in the Upper Room. Suddenly there came a sound from heaven as of a rushing mighty wind, and it filled all the house where they were sitting; and there appeared unto them cloven tongues like as of fire, and it sat upon each of them. And they were all filled with the Holy Spirit. These one hundred twenty disciples were filled with the fire of God and became one hundred twenty messengers of deliverance. God wants you to be filled with the power and presence of God; He wants you to be filled with His fire so you can become a burning bush. God wants you and me to be filled with the fire of God so that you and I become messengers of deliverance.

Moses was the man God had chosen. God never chooses an organization; He finds a man through all the ages. God always has found a man. God will use you, and you, and you; God will use whosoever wants to be used by Him. The reason why God chooses a man or a woman is because He can get his heart and mind; but in a great organization, there are many minds and problems. God can take you and me to bring deliverance and to be obedient to His call.

First, God had the instrument; then the fire; in the third place, the time had come that was the hour of God to deliver His people. The time had come; there were people to be delivered; God had found the man. God said to Moses, "Go and deliver My people; go and give them liberty." The same is true today; millions of people in the whole world are in slavery. Two billion and seventy-five million people are in slavery because they don't know Christ as their Savior; and God says to you and me, "Go and deliver My people; go and put them in freedom." He says to us, "I will give you power and authority. I will send My Spirit upon you. I will cause My power to flow through you. I will enter and live in your soul." Think of that—God descending and making His home in our souls, living in you and me. Listen, friends: if God could enter a bush and speak through it, God can speak through you and me.

Moses made up his mind that he would be a burning bush, that he would have the power and the presence of God. Friends, make up your mind that you want the power of God, make up your mind what you want from God, and if you make up your mind, He will put His power, glory, dominion, and authority in your soul; for with a people who do things half, and don't do it really, God cannot do anything with them. His Word says that obedience is better than sacrifice.

My desire is to have greater power—to be a burning bush. What greater things could a man do than to put his hands on suffering humanity and see the sick healed, the blind eyes opened, the deaf ears opened? That is my desire, to be a burning bush like Moses. When Moses turned aside, God said to him, "I will give you power, I will give you authority, I will send My blessing upon you." Because you stood to listen to the message of the gospel, God will bless you. He will pour in your soul the power of His blessing.

Time Now for the Greatest Revival in History

The time has come for the greatest revival the world has ever known in every nation, tongue, and tribe. God is waiting for you and me to become a burning bush, to have the power of God to deliver the nation and to bring peace to a troubled world. All the peace treaties, cannons, and arms have taken us far away from peace, and there is only One who can bring peace to the world, and that is Jesus! Jesus! Jesus! The Son of God, only the Prince of Peace—only He can bring peace and joy to the troubled soul.

Sin has been the terrible enemy of man. When God made man, He made him a spiritual being; he was crowned with spiritual life, but when sin came into the world—listen to this, please! When sin came into the world, it took away the Spirit from the throne and crowned man with the intellectuality. When sin came into the world, it dethroned the Spirit of God in that man's soul and crowned him with intellectuality. I don't want you to misunderstand me. I am not against intellectuality. Thank God for the intellectuality and the education. I am studying constantly, and we all ought to study, but the Bible says that we must study to be approved by God.[95]

The Pentecostal power converts the man into a spiritual being. He can then act like God, perform miracles like God, and think like God, and that is why God sent the Pentecostal power.

Some of you do not understand the Pentecostal power; there are some that do not believe in the Pentecostal experience. Why did

95. See 2 Timothy 2:15.

God send it? When God made man in the beginning, He gave him power and authority; he could do the things he wanted. He could act and think like God. Then, sin came and robbed the man of all the virtues. On the day of Pentecost, God restored to the man what he had lost at the beginning. You ask me, how did He do it? I tell you how God did it: with the baptism of the Holy Spirit.

How can one think like God? How can one act like God? Now, I don't want you to misunderstand my words: I am speaking of the spiritual man. The reason why God gives you spiritual things is so that you can act spiritually—not with the flesh but with the Spirit of God.

God gave to the man nine spiritual gifts: a word of knowledge, a word of wisdom, discerning of spirits, faith, healings, miracles, prophecy, tongues, interpretation of tongues. God has given us nine spiritual gifts; I can think like God, I can act like God, and I can speak like God.

You ask, how can I do it? The first three gifts are a word of knowledge, a word of wisdom—it does not say knowledge and wisdom—and the discerning of spirits; if you have these three, you can act like God. They are given by the Spirit! It is not anything you can learn; you can't get it out of books, but it comes suddenly, in the twinkle of an eye. God gives it, and I can think like God.

How can I act like God? I can do it when I have the gifts of miracles, faith, and healings; for this is how Jesus worked when He was on the earth. He healed all who came to Him.

So, we have discovered we can think and act like God. How can I speak like God? If I have the Holy Spirit, I can not only speak in other tongues but interpret. I have something greater—I can speak in prophecy; it goes from my soul, it flows under the anointing of the Holy Spirit—the word of prophecy. I can speak like God. That is why we need the baptism of the Holy Spirit. Do you believe it?

We need to stop playing at church. We need to do the things really, not only pray but be obedient to the Word of God and say to God, "I will go wherever You will send me. I will do what You want me to do. I will be what You want me to be."

There are people that are afraid of receiving too much. God will never overpower your will. He will give you what you want. If you want the power and the presence of God, if you want the baptism of the Holy Spirit, He will give it to you.

Bibliography

Barrett, David B., ed. *World Christian Encyclopedia: A Comparative Survey of Churches and Religions in the Modern World*, 2nd ed., vol. 1. New York: Oxford University Press, 2001.

Burgess, Stanley M., and McGee, Gary B. ed. *Dictionary of Pentecostal and Charismatic Movements*. Grand Rapids, MI: Zondervan Publishing House, 1988.

"But What about Hicks?" *The Christian Century* (July 7, 1954): 814–815.

Durasoff, Steve. *Bright Wind of the Spirit: Pentecostalism Today*. Tulsa, OK: Rhema Bible Church, 1972.

Du Plessis, David (as told to Bob Slosser). *A Man Called Mr. Pentecost*. Plainfield, NJ: Logos International, 1977.

———. *Simple and Profound*. Orleans, MA: Paraclete Press, Inc., 1986.

———. *The Spirit Bade Me Go*, rev. ed. Plainfield, NJ: Logos International, 1970.

Frodsham, Stanley Howard. *Smith Wigglesworth: Apostle of Faith*. Springfield, MO: Gospel Publishing House, 1948.

Gibson, Houston. "Tommy Hicks Speaks at Denver Chapter," *Full Gospel Business Men's Voice* (November 1955): 27–29.

Hicks, Tommy (as recorded by Gerald Derstine). "Vision Given to Tommy Hicks, Evangelist, July 25, 1961." Reprinted from *Harvest Time* magazine, n.d.

———. *It's Closing Time, Gentlemen*. Los Angeles: Manifest Deliverance and Worldwide Evangelism, Inc., 1958.

———. *Millions Found Christ: History's Greatest Recorded Revival*. Los Angeles: Manifest Deliverance and Worldwide Evangelism, Inc., 1956.

———. "My Second World-Wide Mission Tour," *Full Gospel Business Men's Voice*, vol. 3, no. 7 (October 1955): 3–18.

Liardon, Roberts. *God's Generals: Why They Succeeded and Why Some Failed*. New Kensington, PA: Whitaker House, 1996.

Nickel, Thomas R. "A Subsequent Report of the Hicks Mission," *Full Gospel Business Men's Voice* (January 1956): 10–16.

Parham, Mrs. Charles. *The Life of Charles Parham*. Birmingham, AL: Commercial Printing Company, 1930.

Robinson, Martin. "To the Ends of the Earth: The Pilgrimage of an Ecumenical Pentecostal, David J. du Plessis (1905–1987)." Ph.D. dissertation: University of Birmingham, England, 1987.

Sandidge, Jerry L. "Roman Catholic/Pentecostal Dialogue: A Contribution to Christian Unity," *Pneuma* 7 (1985): 41–61.

Stokes, Louie W. *The Great Revival in Buenos Aires*. Buenos Aires, Argentina: 1954.

Wigglesworth, Smith. *Ever Increasing Faith*. Springfield, MO: Gospel Publishing House, 1924, 1971.

———. *Smith Wigglesworth Speaks to Students of the Bible*. Compiled by Roberts Liardon. Tulsa, OK: Albury Publishing, 1998.

———. *Smith Wigglesworth: The Complete Collection of His Life Teachings*. Compiled by Roberts Liardon. Tulsa, OK: Albury Publishing, 1996.

About the Compiler

Dr. Roberts Liardon, author, public speaker, spiritual leader, church historian, and humanitarian was born in Tulsa, Oklahoma, the first male child born at Oral Roberts University. For this distinction, he was named in honor of the university founder.

Roberts' career in ministry began at a young age, when in 1979, he gave his first public address at the age of thirteen. Then, at seventeen, he published his first book, *I Saw Heaven*, which catapulted him into the public eye. The book sold over 1.5 million copies and by the following year, Roberts had become one of the leading public speakers in the Christian community all over the world.

Shortly after the publication of *I Saw Heaven*, God inspired Roberts to write and produce a book and video series entitled God's Generals, which chronicled the lives of some of our leading Pentecostal and charismatic leaders. These books included *God's Generals: Why They Succeeded and Why Some Failed*; *God's Generals: The Roaring Reformers*; *God's Generals: The Revivalists*; and *God's Generals: The Healing Evangelists*. The series was an immediate success, establishing Roberts as a leading Protestant church historian.

Since the beginning of the millennium, Roberts has continued to fulfill a demanding speaking schedule along with writing new books and mentoring a new generation of world leaders to effect change for the church and society. He continues to manage and expand his international headquarters in Sarasota, Florida, and has an extension office in London, England.

Roberts Liardon Ministries
US Office:
P.O. Box 2989 • Sarasota, FL 34230

UK and Europe Office:
22 Notting Hill Gate, Suite 125 • London W11 3JE, UK

E-mail: info1@robertsliardon.org • www.RobertsLiardon.com
Facebook: www.facebook.com/RobertsLiardon
Twitter: @RobertsLiardon